SPIRITUAL
Patriots
JUDE'S CALL TO ARMS

SPIRITUAL

Patriots

JUDE'S CALL TO ARMS

AUBREY JOHNSON

Gospel Advocate Company
Nashville, Tennessee

Published by Gospel Advocate Co.
1006 Elm Hill Pike, Nashville, TN 37210
http://www.gospeladvocate.com

ISBN-10: 0-89225-558-7
ISBN-13: 978-0-89225-558-0

TABLE OF CONTENTS

Acknowledgments

Many people have contributed to the publication of this manuscript, but the labors of two are especially noteworthy. I want to thank my former secretary, Tiny Corder, and my brother-in-law, Dr. Matt Hearn, for their help in making *Spiritual Patriots* a much better book than I was capable of producing alone.

Dedication

To Neil and Kerry Anderson with grateful appreciation
for your courageous defense of the once delivered faith.

INTRODUCTION
Courage of Steel

Patriots are people who passionately love their country and are willing to support and defend it with their very lives. The word "patriot" awakens memories of great heroes from America's military history. There was Patrick Henry who declared, "Give me liberty, or give me death!" Or who could ever forget Nathan Hale's declaration from the gallows, "I only regret that I have but one life to lose for my country." Names like Alvin York, Audie Murphy, "Stormin" Norman Schwarzkopf and Tommy Franks demand our respect and gratitude for their selflessness and bravery.

That same kind of devotion can be seen in the lives of early Christians. Peter and John were beaten and commanded not to teach or preach in the name of Jesus. Although threatened with prison and death, they did not cease to proclaim the gospel. Paul was persecuted at every turn yet never shied away from his duty. Stephen was stoned and James was beheaded for their uncompromising loyalty to Christ. Physical persecution is rare in American culture, but Christians must be no less determined to withstand the world and advance the kingdom of God.

Christians are soldiers of Christ on active duty. As citizens of heaven, they long for their homeland and readily acknowledge their status as pilgrims and sojourners in this present world. One day in the future,

Jesus will return to withdraw His troops from this temporary tour of duty called "life." Until that time, the church serves as His outpost on earth. That colony of heaven cannot be defined geographically, but it is no less real. The Lord reigns in the hearts of men and women who have been redeemed by His Son.

God's patriots are faithful saints who deeply love the church and have pledged to support and defend it with a resolve reminiscent of that displayed by George Washington during the American Revolutionary War. Ours is a spiritual revolution. At conversion, Christians declare their liberty from Satan and loyalty to God. The devil, like King George, will not release his former subjects without a battle. Christians are in for the fight of their lives; only the committed will survive the on-slaughts of the enemy.

The book of Jude is God's field manual for spiritual engagement and His call to arms. It reminds us that our adversary is real and determined. It tells us how to respond to the world's hostility and aggression. There is no room for pacifism or appeasement when eternity is at stake! It is a life-and-death struggle for the souls of men and women. Christians must not lose their will to fight the good fight! May God bless you with courage of steel and a heart of peace as you prepare for the battle ahead.

ONE
Spiritual Sentries

Jude 1-2

If I am to know victory, I must be willing to take a stand.

The book of Jude was intended to serve a twofold purpose. It was both a heavenly call to arms and a strategy for spiritual victory in the good fight of faith. Success depended on the willingness of Christians to heed God's wake-up call and face the reality that false teachers had infiltrated their ranks and posed a serious threat to the well-being of the church.

When trouble arises, it is not enough to sit idly by and wish things were different. Like a deadly disease, the problem cannot be corrected by ignoring it and hoping it will go away. With many illnesses, there is a brief but precious window of opportunity to treat the malady and stop its progress. The same is true in opposing the spread of harmful teaching. Jude understood that time was of the essence, and he was determined to rally the troops and make the most of the opportunity heaven afforded them. Under the guidance of the Holy Spirit, he urged them to unite and fight.

If they would band together and withstand the proponents of error, it was not too late to halt the injurious effects of the false teachers' influence. But if they failed to come together, the consequences of their cowardice would be inestimable. Although God was certain to prevail in the end, the loss and suffering would be unspeakable (Esther 4:14).

In addition to alerting them to danger, Jude's letter served as a field manual for battling false teaching in an effective and godly manner. A field manual is different from a novel or classroom textbook. It is not filled with unproven theories and ivory-tower philosophy. It is concise and practical. Such a book is designed for the battlefield, not the living room.

The book of Jude is God's field manual for saints whose faith and values have come under fire. It was written to provide guidance for Christians struggling against growing worldliness in the church. It contains down-to-earth advice for spiritual patriots battling unbiblical change that would destroy the identity of God's people. The author of this potent little instruction manual was a man by the name of Jude.

DOUBTER TO DEFENDER

Jude was raised in a Jewish family in Nazareth of Galilee in the first century A.D. His parents, Joseph and Mary, were poor but proud descendants of David from the tribe of Judah. In many ways, they resembled a typical Israelite family, but they were anything but typical.

Mary's first child, Jesus, was born under the most amazing circumstances. It began with the visit of an angel named Gabriel. The heavenly messenger announced that Mary, although still a virgin, would give birth to a child who would be called the Son of God. Her conception would be accomplished miraculously by the overshadowing of the Holy Spirit.

After Jesus' birth in Bethlehem of Judea, the family eventually returned to Nazareth. Many children were added to the home through the natural relations of a husband and wife united in marriage. The sons included James, Joses, Simon and Jude (Matthew 13:55-56).

When Jesus was about 30 years old, He began preaching publicly and soon rose to national prominence. A spectacular healing ministry accompanied His teaching and reinforced His message. The half brothers of Jesus struggled along with the rest of the Jewish population to account for His powerful words and works.

Jesus became very popular with the common people, and many gladly recognized Him as the promised Messiah. The religious leaders, however, felt threatened by His growing fame and attempted to discredit Him by linking His miracles to Satan (Mark 3:22). During three years of public ministry, Jesus dramatically demonstrated His divinity, yet His brothers still did not believe in Him (John 7:3-5).

The resurrection of Jesus appears to have initiated a great change in His family. After Christ's ascension into heaven from the Mount of Olives, they can be found joining in prayer with the apostles and faithful women while awaiting the promise of the Father (Acts 1:14). That prayer was answered on Pentecost when the Holy Spirit arrived and equipped the Twelve to be effective witnesses for Jesus (v. 8; 2:1-4). Three thousand people gladly received their words and were baptized that very day for the forgiveness of sins (vv. 38-41).

Although not apostles, the brothers of Jesus received significant roles in the growing movement. Jesus appeared to James after the resurrection, and James quickly rose to become a pillar in the church (1 Corinthians 15:7; Galatians 2:9). Jude, although younger, also played an active part in those early days. Evidence suggests that he was a traveling missionary whose wife accompanied and aided him in his ministry (1 Corinthians 9:5). At some point during his work, he wrote a letter that has since become known as the book of Jude. God saw fit to preserve that inspired epistle for the benefit of Christians in future generations.

A SUMMARY OF JUDE'S LETTER

Jude's writing followed the common form of letters in the first century. He began with a signature, identifying himself as the author. Next came the address where he named those to whom he wrote. This was followed by a salutation, expressing his prayerful wish for their well-being. In the body of the letter, he explained his reason for writing and followed it up with practical instruction.

The purpose of Jude's epistle was to sound an urgent warning against emerging worldliness in the church. The disciples were charged to contend for the faith with all the courage they could muster. Their morale was bolstered by Jude's confidence that the false teachers troubling the church would not succeed in the end. He carefully explained how Christians should conduct themselves during this time of crisis and closed the letter with a beautiful benediction, assuring the faithful of God's ability to sustain them through the struggles they were encountering.

THE AUTHOR

Readers cannot help appreciating Jude from the opening line of his letter. Despite his unusual relationship to Christ, he refused to exploit it for personal advantage. Two phrases sum up his humble self-identity.

• **Brother of James.** Jude was happy to be known as the "brother of James." His sibling was far more famous, but Jude accepted his less visible role without any resentment. Not only did he allow others to refer to him in this way, but he also graciously did so himself.

The Bible is filled with examples of men who are highly regarded because they were content to be second in the public eye. Consider Jonathan, crown prince and heir to the throne of Israel, who was willing to see David sit in his place if God so desired it. John the Baptist freely accepted the decline in his own following because he knew it meant more disciples for the Lord. Although an apostle in his own right, Andrew was content to be known as Simon Peter's brother.

A person cannot exalt Christ and self at the same time. Humility is repulsive to the worldly mind, but it is a spiritual quality to be highly prized by those who seek their praise from God. Jesus' words must have echoed in Jude's mind: "And whoever exalts himself will be humbled, and he who humbles himself will be exalted" (Matthew 23:12). Those who are wise allow the Lord to lift them up rather than promoting themselves (James 4:10).

• **Bondservant of Jesus Christ.** "Servant" was the other word Jude used to identify himself. Although some people seek worldly titles to impress others with their authority, the Bible's great leaders have shown a preference for the more modest label, "servant." This humble designation reflected their understanding that they were representing God and not themselves. Jude wanted his readers to be absolutely clear that his message was from and for Christ.

In Jude's estimation, there was no higher post he could aspire to than being the Lord's servant. What loftier goal could he pursue than to hear at life's completion, "Well done, good and faithful servant; you were faithful over a few things, I will make you ruler over many things. Enter into the joy of your lord" (Matthew 25:21)? Jude understood that a man's importance in this world comes from what he can do for others, not what he has the power to make others do for him (23:11). That is why heaven belongs to those who find joy in servanthood while here on earth.

THE RECIPIENTS

It is difficult to pinpoint precisely when, where and to whom Jude wrote his epistle. What is known about the document's recipients is that they were "called," "sanctified" and "preserved." These words graphically describe what it means to be a Christian.

• **Called.** Through the gospel God's call is extended to all people (2 Thessalonians 2:13-14). The Lord endowed human beings with the freedom to choose whether to accept His gracious offer of abundant life (Mark 16:15-16). Those who embrace the gospel should realize they have been called to holiness and service as well as to forgiveness. A Christian's entire lifetime should be dedicated to making that calling and election sure (2 Peter 1:10).

• **Sanctified.** The ground of this calling is the love that prompted God to take the initiative in man's salvation. Paul rejoiced that, "God demonstrates His own love toward us, in that while we were still sinners, Christ died for us" (Romans 5:8). All people are loved by God and therefore called, but there is a special sense in which those who accept that call are His "beloved" (Jude 1 NASB). Contemplating the wonder of that relationship led John to exult "Behold what manner of love the Father has bestowed on us, that we should be called children of God!" (1 John 3:1).

Those who embrace the Father's love are sanctified by Him. The summons to be set apart is initiated by divine love. The acceptance of heaven's invitation is confirmed by human love expressed in submission to God's commands. Sanctification involves growth in Christlikeness; and growth in Christlikeness requires increasing one's ability to give and receive love.

• **Preserved.** When a person responds appropriately to the gospel call, he is kept in Jesus. Those who are outside Christ will perish, but

those who are in Christ will be preserved from eternal death. A person
who is baptized into Christ (Romans 6:3; Galatians 3:27) must also
abide in Jesus to be kept eternally (John 15:4-6).

Saints show their love for Christ by keeping His commandments,
and those who love Him are kept by Him. All of heaven's resources are
available to help Christians grow spiritually and live faithfully. If a person is lost, it will not be due to Christ's carelessness, the Spirit's stingi-
ness, or the Father's failure to love and protect. It will be a breakdown
of his own heart (Revelation 2:4; 2 Thessalonians 2:9-12; James 4:4).

THE PRAYER

Jude concluded the introduction to his letter with a sincere prayer
for the spiritual well-being of his readers. Three things were specifically requested in their behalf: mercy, peace and love. In conjunc-
tion with writing, Jude saw prayer as a means to multiply these virtues
and promote a more loving atmosphere in this deeply troubled church.
His desire was for these blessings to increase until they overflowed
in their midst.

In Jude's letter, the word "mercy" appears in place of "grace," which
is more common in the New Testament epistles. The meaning is similar
and calls for a readiness to forgive the wrongs of others as one grows
in awareness of how much he has been forgiven in Christ (Ephesians
4:30-32). Where mercy abounds, the possibility of peace also expands.

Another unique feature of Jude's salutation was his earnest plea
for an increase of love. From all that follows in his letter, it is clear that
Jude's idea of love was robust and redemptive rather than weak and
sentimental. Love does not mean ignoring problems and pretending
they do not exist. True love faces troubles and seeks to solve them.
Jude's love led him to battle false teachers and proves that opposing
doctrinal error and exposing its promoters is a courageous and com-
mendable form of love.

Compassion and confrontation are not mutually exclusive. In fact,
avoiding conflict at all costs is the antithesis of love because it ex-
poses the most vulnerable to needless danger. A caring parent who ob-
serves a poisonous snake near his child's favorite play area will warn
the child and remove the snake. Failure to do so is heartless and irre-

sponsible. Love guards the object of its concern whether the threat is physical or spiritual.

THE PURPOSE

After a pleasant introduction, the time had come to alert the saints to the danger threatening their spiritual security. The service Jude rendered was like that of a watchman ever on guard against a city's approaching enemies. In this case, the trumpet was sounded in the 11th hour after the opposition had already infiltrated the community of believers.

This scenario calls to mind the work of Ezekiel, who was appointed by God to serve as a spiritual watchman over the house of Israel. In Ezekiel 3:17-21, the Lord gave him these instructions:

> Son of man, I have made you a watchman for the house of Israel; therefore hear a word from My mouth, and give them warning from Me: When I say to the wicked, "You shall surely die," and you give him no warning, nor speak to warn the wicked from his wicked way, to save his life, that same wicked man shall die in his iniquity; but his blood I will require at your hand. Yet, if you warn the wicked, and he does not turn from his wickedness, nor from his wicked way, he shall die in his iniquity; but you have delivered your soul. Again, when a righteous man turns from his righteousness and commits iniquity, and I lay a stumbling block before him, he shall die; because you did not give him warning, he shall die in his sin, and his righteousness which he has done shall not be remembered; but his blood I will require at your hand. Nevertheless if you warn the righteous man that the righteous should not sin, and he does not sin, he shall surely live because he took warning; also you will have delivered your soul.

A watchman was accountable with his own life for the faithful discharge of his duty. Both Ezekiel and Jude valiantly accomplished their missions.

As in Jude's day, the world continues its encroachment into the church. Satan has continually refined his tactics until worldliness appears more respectable and false teaching more plausible than ever before. The church is still in need of courageous men and women who will confront the error and immorality that jeopardize the body of Christ. Who will fearlessly oppose sin instead of sitting by and watching its virulent spread?

During the time of Ezekiel, the Lord searched for a man who would stand in the gap and halt the moral and spiritual collapse of His people (Ezekiel 22:30). Jude was just such a man in his day. Where are the watchmen of our own generation who, in humility and love, will stand and be counted for truth?

DISCUSSION

1. Why was it difficult for Jesus' brothers to believe in Him?

2. Describe the basic parts of a letter in the first century.

3. What is significant about Jude's reference to himself as James' brother?

4. Why is heaven reserved for those who discover the joy of servanthood here on earth?

5. What did Jude mean when he referred to his readers as "called"?

6. How are Christians God's beloved in distinction from humanity in general? How are love and sanctification linked?

7. What does it mean to be "preserved" or "kept" in Jesus?

8. How can prayer multiply mercy, peace and love in the church?

9. What was the occasion of Jude's letter?

10. How can Jude be compared to a watchman in ancient times? Why does that work need to be continued today?

TWO

A Patriotic Plea

Jude 3

*If I am to know victory, I must adapt my plans
to fulfill greater needs.*

I n the heat of battle, the best laid plans may have to be changed at
a moment's notice. A flanking maneuver by the enemy calls for
quick realignment. An ambush requires instantaneous adjustment.
Jude's rapid response to a crisis confronting the church demonstrates
that spiritual battle is no different.

The book of Jude has a military ring throughout. The author was a
model leader in the Lord's army. He cared deeply for the soldiers of
Christ who fought daily on the front lines in defense of truth. The motive behind each inspired command was genuine concern for their well-
being. The warmth of their fellowship united and sustained them in
their struggles against Satan.

PLAN A — APPRECIATE THE GOSPEL

To fortify the faith of his friends, Jude had intended to write to them
about their common salvation. The word "common" does not refer to

something that is ordinary. Jude used it to accentuate the universality of the gospel: it is for all people regardless of worldly distinctions (John 3:16; 1 Timothy 2:4); it is available to every human being on the same terms (Galatians 3:26-28); it places each Christian under obligation to obey the Lord with complete devotion (2 Timothy 2:4; Hebrews 5:9); and it offers the same reward of eternal life to all who remain faithful (1 John 2:25). God does not play favorites with select groups or individuals. In a world of double standards, it is nice to know that there is equality in Jesus Christ.

Jude's strategy was praiseworthy, but circumstances forced him to alter his course after learning that his friends were under attack from false teachers. He felt constrained to lay aside his plan and write about what was more needful. One cannot help sympathizing with Jude as the crisis compelled him to undertake a less pleasant assignment.

Did Jude ever find time to complete his treatise on salvation? Perhaps that need was met by Paul's epistle to the Romans. Regardless, what must have seemed like an irritating interruption was, in actuality, God overruling. By redirecting Jude's writing, the Lord filled a special niche in the canon of Scripture. The book of Jude has been a continual source of strength for Christians who find their faith under fire.

In the story of the good Samaritan, Jesus reminded His followers always to be open to the needful (Luke 10:30-37). The priest and Levite refused to change their preset plans and missed a moment of greater opportunity. The Samaritan interrupted his personal schedule when compassion required it and was commended by the Lord.

Jesus was always ready to be "troubled." The disciples seemed ever aware of pressing appointments to be met that allowed no time for distractions like "bothersome" women (Matthew 15:21-28) or children (Mark 10:13-14). Jesus welcomed these interruptions as the essence of real living. From the divine perspective, human needs are never inconveniences.

PLAN B — DEFEND THE GOSPEL
Jude did not relate how he learned about the crisis his readers were facing. Regardless of the source, the disturbing news was that a group of professed Christians had identified with the church and had begun

circulating heretical teaching. The doctrinal error they were advancing would require urgent action to halt its harmful effects.

Jude's desire was to write about the wonderful salvation Christians have in Jesus. Circumstances demanded that he alter his well-intentioned plan and exhort his readers to *defend* the gospel rather than merely *appreciate* it. This challenge implies the presence of opposition. The gospel has had its enemies from the very beginning. Some work from without to overthrow it, while others operate from within to undermine it. When adversaries grow bold enough to launch such an offensive, Christians must be prepared to respond.

It is always more enjoyable to talk about the beauty of Christianity than to unmask false teaching, but heresy cannot be allowed to go unopposed. A patriot would much rather be at home with his wife and children than in combat, but if necessary, he will risk his life in their defense. So the church must have its spiritual patriots who will fight the good fight and defend the church from its enemies. No sensible person likes conflict, but when God's Word is under attack and souls are at stake, Christians must take their stand. There is no place for spiritual pacifism when evil is advancing.

If a woman was being mugged and a policeman refused to aid her until he completed the traffic ticket he was writing, the public would be outraged. Or if a child was seriously injured and the only available doctor refused to treat him until he finished his rounds, he would be dismissed for negligence. When a crisis occurs, priorities must change. This principle holds true not only in health care but also in soul care. Churches cannot conduct business as usual when the faith of members is under attack and eternity hangs in the balance. Time and attention must be immediately redirected to the need at hand.

THE POWER OF EXHORTATION

Jude began his counteroffensive by writing a letter. Writing has been an important Christian ministry since the first century. It continues to be a vital means of communication and edification today. Cards and letters can encourage, remind, instruct or, as in this case, exhort.

Jude's intent was not to provide a lot of new instruction. His purpose was to urge his hearers to heed what they had already received. If they were to survive, he must awaken them from their spiritual slumber and prepare them for the upcoming skirmish. Words are powerful tools to be used for good or evil. To exhort means to warn, advise or encourage by use of words. The Greeks used this term to depict a general issuing orders to his army.

Christians are under orders to encourage one another with regularity: "[B]ut exhort one another daily, while it is called 'Today,' lest any of you be hardened through the deceitfulness of sin" (Hebrews 3:13). The Hebrews writer seems to have envisioned a spontaneous process in which saints call on each other to resist temptation and withstand trial as the situation warrants. Holding each other accountable would protect their consciences from losing their spiritual sensitivity. Sin must not be allowed to escalate without timely intervention.

The focus of Jude's exhortation was to alert his readers to the world's intrusion into the church. He encouraged them to contend for the faith before it was too late. If they did not act quickly, the church would be lost to the false teachers who had penetrated their fellowship.

THE ONCE DELIVERED FAITH

"The faith" Jude mentions does not refer to an individual's subjective belief in Jesus or the gospel. This is made clear by Jude's reference to its being "delivered." Instead, it is an objective body of teaching of which Jesus is both source and subject. It is the sum of all that Christians are to believe and do. Jesus' ethical teachings and religious instructions are vital parts of the faith that grow out of a proper understanding of His divine nature and work upon the cross.

It is crucial for Christians to understand that they have a revealed faith. The gospel was not concocted by ambitious, self-serving men; nor was it the result of a humanistic evolutionary process: it was delivered for a reason (1 Corinthians 1:21; Galatians 1:11-12). That body of teaching was carefully recorded and now constitutes what is known as the New Testament. It was first revealed by Jesus and then by His inspired messengers (Hebrews 2:3-4). The Holy Spirit gave them a full recollection of all that Jesus said and guided them into all truth (John 14:26; 16:13).

Jude placed strong emphasis on the faith being *once* delivered. False teachers were attempting to corrupt the gospel by claiming they possessed special knowledge that justified their worldly ways. Jude reminded his readers that the truth entrusted to their care was both perfect and permanent. The message they received was never to be annulled, superseded or amended. It was delivered once for all time. The faith was revealed by Christ, delivered orally by the apostles, and gradually committed to writing by inspired men. The New Testament is God's final revelation to man. Even before the canon was complete, Christians in Jude's day had a recognizable body of teaching that was identified as "the faith" (Galatians 1:23; Acts 6:7). The exclusive content of that teaching was reflected in John's warning, "Whoever transgresses and does not abide in the doctrine of Christ does not have God. He who abides in the doctrine of Christ has both the Father and the Son" (2 John 9). Similarly, Paul declared, "As we have said before, so now I say again, if anyone preaches any other gospel to you than what you have received, let him be accursed" (Galatians 1:9).

THE CALL TO CONTEND

Because the gospel could never be transcended by new teaching, Jude urged his readers to contend for the faith. He was convinced that guarding that message from those who would corrupt it was one of the few things worth fighting for in life. God's patriots should be concerned about soundness in the faith (Titus 1:13), personally stand fast in the faith (1 Corinthians 16:13), and be prepared to defend or "contend for" the faith (Jude 3).

The word "contend" is an athletic term that means to wrestle or put forth great effort. The English word "agonize" is derived from it. Jude was saying that Christians should spare no effort to uphold truth. They are to put up a real fight against false teaching, giving it their all.

That wholesome charge must never be confused with physical or verbal abuse. Peter was prepared to fight to the death for Jesus but was rebuked by the Master for cutting off the ear of Malchus, servant of the High Priest (John 18:10-11). At His trial, the Lord told Pilate, "My kingdom is not of this world. If My kingdom were of this world, My servants would fight, so that I should not be delivered to the Jews; but now My kingdom is not from here" (v. 36).

The only fighting Jesus' servants are to engage in is spiritual in nature. Paul wrote, "For the weapons of our warfare are not carnal but mighty in God for pulling down strongholds, casting down arguments and every high thing that exalts itself against the knowledge of God, bringing every thought into captivity to the obedience of Christ" (2 Corinthians 10:4-5). Christians are to battle for people's hearts and minds. With God's Word as their sword (Ephesians 6:17), they defend truth and wage relentless war against falsehood.

Jude's words clearly emphasize that doctrine does matter (1 Timothy 1:3; Romans 16:17). Unfortunately, many religious teachers are minimizing the importance of Christ's teaching while exalting a kind of vague faith based on emotion rather than biblical truth. Faith and love are of utmost importance in Christianity, but the true nature of these virtues has been distorted beyond recognition by many theologians and preachers.

What should be done about false teachers in view of the primacy of love among God's people? Rather than compromising God's Word for the sake of artificial unity, real love demands that loyal Christians contend for the faith! This is the duty of elders and evangelists (Titus 1:9; 3:10), but maintaining the purity of the gospel is the sacred trust of every faithful Christian. It is a personal call to speak up in behalf of truth in one's circle of influence. Those who love Jesus, His church and lost souls can do no less.

"Earnestly" is the word used by Jude to modify the duty of defending the faith. Saints must fight for truth fervently with all their might (Titus 2:15). A carefree attitude in the struggle against error is sure to end in defeat.

In commenting about a personal confrontation he had with false teachers, Paul wrote, "[W]e did not yield submission even for an hour, that the truth of the gospel might continue with you" (Galatians 2:5). Victory demands a willingness to fight hardily for truth while maintaining a Christlike demeanor at all times. Speaking the truth in love is the secret to contending without being contentious (Ephesians 4:15).

A TRUST TO KEEP

The faith is like a baton being handed from one runner to the next in a relay race. It is similar to the Olympic torch transferred between athletes as they carry it to the stadium for the beginning of the games. As truth is passed down from one generation to the next, there comes with it the duty to protect and preserve it.

When thoughtful people reflect on the price others have paid to safeguard the purity of the gospel, it ought to make them tremble. More importantly, it should motivate them to take their place in the fight against worldliness. Although saints should never go looking for trouble or battle over petty personal differences, they must always be prepared to withstand the enemies of Christ. Those who do so can take their stand with Paul and declare, "I have fought the good fight, I have finished the race, I have kept the faith" (2 Timothy 4:7).

DISCUSSION

1. What did Jude mean by the expression "common salvation"?

2. How valuable is writing as a Christian ministry today?

3. Why is it important for Christians to be able to adapt to changing needs and circumstances?

4. Is there anything worth fighting for in life?

5. What is the importance of exhortation?

6. Explain the meaning of the phrase "the faith."

7. What does it mean that the faith was "once for all delivered"?

8. Why is earnestness important when contending for the faith?

9. How can Christians contend for the faith without being contentious?

10. How is contending for the faith an act of love?

THREE

Slipping in Secretly

Jude 4

---

*If I am to know victory, I must never use grace
as an excuse for disobedience.*

"Treason" is a word that arouses strong emotions in citizens of any country. What constitutes treason varies from nation to nation, but there is universal contempt for it. Death and life imprisonment are two of the most common ways of punishing this serious crime. Unfortunately, the problem of treason is not limited to political governments. Jude wrote to warn his brothers in Christ of spiritual sedition within the kingdom of God.

False teachers had slipped into the congregation of which Jude's readers were a part. It was not their physical presence that was secretive but their true beliefs, motives and intentions. They passed themselves off as faithful Christians, but they were only pretenders. Like double agents, they worked to subvert the very faith they professed.

WAKE UP, SHEPHERDS!

The fact that these men crept in unnoticed is a solemn reminder that guardians of the flock shoulder a serious responsibility. Jude implied that if the elders had been aware of the dangerous doctrines these false teachers planned to promote, they would have stopped them in the beginning. Now that these men had established a following, it would be far more difficult to silence them (Titus 1:9-11). Elders must not become complacent and go to sleep at their posts. Church leaders must make it their business to know what is being taught in their congregations. Paul cautioned the Ephesian elders to be on the lookout for false teachers who would emerge from within their fellowship (Acts 20:28-32). The apostle advised them to immerse themselves in Scripture so they would be able to recognize and withstand religious error when it surfaced.

An important part of shepherding is guarding the flock from predators. That is why doctrinal interviews are an indispensable part of hiring preachers and youth ministers. Not even volunteer ministry leaders should be selected indiscriminately. Bible school teachers and youth workers should be appointed with great care.

Responsible elderships make it a point to get acquainted with all new members. There are times when it is beneficial to communicate with the churches they formerly attended. Most Christians appreciate their shepherds' desire to get to know them personally and respect their leaders' desire to preserve the peace and security of the congregation. Sensible saints understand that elders are men of goodwill who are not motivated by suspicion but by a genuine concern for the welfare of souls entrusted to their care. An elder's love is accompanied by a sobering awareness of his accountability before God for safeguarding His flock.

Those who know that their teachings are objectionable to elders are not always forthright about their beliefs and may operate underhandedly to advance their positions. Because false teachers perceive themselves to be more knowledgeable than those they seek to enlighten, they do not equate their lack of candidness with dishonesty. They believe their deception is harmless and justified. No announcement of their intentions will be made at the outset, and no confession of wrongdoing will be made if they are ousted.

THE NEED FOR VIGILANCE

• **A Warning From Jesus.** The Bible is filled with warnings about the battle that must be fought against false teaching. In the Sermon on

the Mount, Jesus said, "Beware of false prophets, who come to you
in sheep's clothing, but inwardly they are ravenous wolves" (Matthew
7:15). "Ravenous" is an adjective meaning fierce or savage. Jesus used
this modifier to describe the inner nature of spiritual fiends who mas-
querade as members of the flock. This inward depravity stands in strik-
ing contrast to the pleasing personality they manifest outwardly. Their
enchanting demeanor allows them rapidly to gain goodwill they do not
deserve. They charm susceptible saints with their smiles and smooth
words and catch them off guard.

• **Warnings From Paul.** Paul had much to say about false teachers
in his letters to Timothy. In the first epistle he warned, "Now the Spirit
expressly says that in latter times some will depart from the faith, giving heed to deceiving spirits and doctrines of demons, speaking lies in
hypocrisy, having their own conscience seared with a hot iron" (1 Timothy 4:1-2). In his second letter, he commanded Timothy to "Preach
the word! Be ready in season and out of season. Convince, rebuke, exhort, with all longsuffering and teaching. For the time will come when
they will not endure sound doctrine, but according to their own desires,
because they have itching ears, they will heap up for themselves teachers; and they will turn their ears away from the truth, and be turned
aside to fables" (2 Timothy 4:2-4).

AN INSIDE JOB

The most disturbing thing about false teachers is that they do their
damage from the inside. In carnal or spiritual warfare, the most dangerous enemies are always those who work from within. That is why
Paul reminded the Corinthians of Satan's ability to transform his servants into ministers of righteousness (2 Corinthians 11:15 KJV). John
advised Christians not to accept self-proclaimed religious leaders without first getting to know them (1 John 4:1). False teachers often have
charismatic personalities and are skilled in the art of spiritual seduc-
tion. A person should always explore the biblical accuracy of teaching
before embracing it.

Luke's commendation of the Bereans for examining Paul's preaching in the light of Scripture proves that the effort to establish authority for Christian beliefs and practices should never be belittled as an un-

spiritual enterprise (Acts 17:11). Diligent study is needed to discern the truth, especially because false teachers are proficient at using Scripture deceptively (Galatians 1:6-7; 2 Corinthians 2:17; 2 Peter 3:16). Paul urged believers to, "Test all things; hold fast what is good" (1 Thessalonians 5:21).

THE FUTURE OF THE UNGODLY

There are many predictions in Scripture of what will ultimately happen to false teachers. Those who pervert God's Word are prophetically consigned to doom. Jude may have had a particular passage in mind (2 Peter 3:3-7; Matthew 24:37-39), or he may have been thinking of God's dealings with disobedient people throughout the Old Testament generally. Those narratives are unmistakable warnings of what transgressors can expect in any age. Judgment and condemnation are divine appointments for the spiritually defiant.

Jude described these false teachers as "ungodly" men in verse 4. The word "ungodly" is used six times in this brief letter to depict those who do not have proper respect for God. Because of their lack of reverence for the Lord and for sacred things in general, they did not hesitate to speak disparagingly of treasured tenets of the faith.

Righteous character begins with the fear of the Lord. Godliness is a positive virtue that encourages men and women to order their lives by the Bible. It provides a healthy frame of reference for making responsible choices in life. Godliness instills a deep desire to hear the Creator's commendation on the day of judgment. It is an attitude of awe rather than terror. It is comparable to the mixture of love and respect children have for good parents. The heavenly Father deserves no less from His children.

TWISTING GRACE

Jude warned that these religious impostors were turning the grace of God into "lewdness." Paul listed lewdness among the works of the flesh that would keep a person out of heaven (Galatians 5:19), and these men were twisting God's words, making them appear to encourage unholy behavior among believers. They justified their immorality by blurring the line between liberty and license. They flaunted their shameless ways and welcomed others to imitate their wantonness.

The relationship between divine grace and human works has been a matter of discussion from the first century until now. Some would suggest that obedience is irrelevant because sinners are saved by the unmerited favor of God. The fact that people are judged according to their works disproves such a theory (Matthew 25:21; Romans 2:6; 2 Corinthians 5:10). There is a definite relationship between one's earthly life and eternal destiny.

What then is the role of man's obedience in the plan of salvation? Paul made it plain that no person is good enough to merit God's favor (Galatians 2:16). James, on the other hand, argued that man cannot be justified without works that correspond to faith (James 2:14-26). Although obedience can never earn salvation, it is a part of God's means to access deliverance and maintain fellowship with Him (Hebrews 12:14). Freedom in Christ does not come without responsibilities. Even grace has its obligations.

The Bible clearly sets forth specific requirements for receiving forgiveness of past sins. Without faith (Mark 16:15-16), repentance (Acts 2:38), confession (Romans 10:10), and baptism (Acts 22:16), there is no promise of cleansing from sin. No man can do enough to deserve salvation, but his faith must express itself in obedience to receive the benefits made available through the death, burial and resurrection of Christ.

Submission to a condition of salvation cannot be equated with conceited attempts to earn salvation. Yielding to baptism is a confession of one's inability to save himself; a clear admission of the need for a Savior; a declaration of faith in Christ's righteousness over self-righteousness.

COMMITMENT VS. QUOTAS

Although the New Testament demands a life of holiness and service from those who seek eternal life (Matthew 25:34-46; Hebrews 12:14; James 1:27), production quotas and sinless perfection are not the issue. At his very best, a Christian is no more than an unprofitable servant (Luke 17:10). Still, there is a real sense in which works are critical to perfect the faith that saves.

The relationship between grace and works will always be somewhat of a mystery to man. It seems that this is an intentional part of God's plan to test human hearts and prove the sincerity of faith. There is a special chemistry between grace and works that keeps a man striving while preventing him from despairing. It is not a question of doing enough but of bringing one's heart into submission to God. Heaven is not a hall of fame for spiritual superstars. God wants surrender, not statistics.

LIBERTY NOT LICENSE

Jude was concerned that new leaders were emerging in the church who misrepresented the grace of God and made it seem to support a worldly lifestyle. They felt no need to hide their sins or to resist temptation. From their perspective, if God's grace covered sin, then Christians could sin without regard to future consequences.

Paul confronted this confused reasoning in his letter to the Romans. Some were suggesting that saints should deliberately sin so God would have even greater opportunity to display His marvelous grace (Romans 6:1). The apostle was shocked that Christians could think that way.

God's grace has been sorely misunderstood and abused over the centuries. Those who use divine mercy to dismiss their sins lightly make a terrible mistake (Romans 6:23). God's gift of eternal life through Jesus Christ is offered graciously – but conditionally – upon death to sin. Grace will forgive sin, but it will never minimize sin.

The apostles were careful to address this point and remove any possibility of confusion. Paul said, "For you, brethren, have been called to liberty; only do not use liberty as an opportunity for the flesh, but through love serve one another" (Galatians 5:13). Peter instructed his readers not to use liberty as a cloak for vice (1 Peter 2:16). John declared, "In this the children of God and the children of the devil are manifest: Whoever does not practice righteousness is not of God, nor is he who does not love his brother" (1 John 3:10). Despite such plain teaching, there have always been men willing to promote worldliness in the name of grace. The problem is not with their minds, but their hearts. The issue is not comprehension, but submission.

DENYING JESUS

Jude charged the false teachers with denying the only Lord God and
the Lord Jesus Christ. People can deny Christ by their words or by their
way of life. When Peter denied the Lord, he claimed no knowledge of
Jesus. When these men denied Him, they were probably claiming a higher knowledge of Jesus. Although professing to know Christ intimately, their doctrine and conduct contradicted their assertion (Titus 1:16).

Those who make intellectual attempts to divorce the spirit and body
are involved in a futile effort to justify their sins. Although one's inner
condition is God's primary concern, it is misleading to say that nothing else matters. Jesus explained that there is an inseparable link between the way a person thinks and the way he acts. Behavior can always be traced back to the heart from which it originated (Matthew
15:16-20). That means sin in the body is an outgrowth of iniquity in
the heart. Thoughts and deeds are a single entity manifested in two
forms (5:28).

SPIRITUAL DISSIDENTS

Spiritual dissidents are always looking for opportunities to infiltrate
peaceful churches and sow seeds of discord. Congregational leaders
must be vigilant in safeguarding their flocks against troublemakers.
Heresies, like those Jude confronted, continue to surface today. Those
who belittle obedience in the name of grace are false teachers. Grace
does not nullify the commandments of God or the sinfulness of immorality. At the same time, care must be shown not to deprecate God's
loving mercy. It will cover any sin when a person genuinely seeks
His forgiveness and submits to His will.

DISCUSSION

1. What emotions do you experience when you hear the word "treason"?

2. What did Jude mean when he said certain men had "crept in unnoticed"?

3. What can elders do to guard against false teaching in the church?

4. Why are enemies more powerful when they work from within rather than without?

5. How had God foretold the doom of the men responsible for troubling the church?

6. How many times did Jude use the term "ungodly"? What does it mean?

7. Define "lewdness."

8. How is it possible to turn grace into lewdness?

9. Describe the relationship between grace and obedience.

10. In what ways might a person deny Jesus as Lord and Christ?

Things Worth Remembering

Jude 5-7

If I am to know victory, I must learn from history.

---

oldiers learn by repetition. In the American Army, servicemen receive their initial instruction under the supervision of a drill sergeant. During basic training, he will require them to repeat exercises designed to help them master the skills of warfare. The idea is to rehearse these abilities until they become instinctive and cannot be forgotten under the stressful conditions of combat.

REPETITION AND READINESS

Well-trained troops do not panic when they come under fire. Their state of readiness is evidenced by their ability to stay calm under intense pressure. Soldiers who dread the demanding routine of boot camp come to see its wisdom when conflict erupts. Soldiers of Christ are no different. If God's patriots are to keep their composure in the midst of crisis, there are certain ideas that must be ingrained in their hearts and minds. The certainty of judgment is one of them.

Although home life is different from military life, they are similar in at least one respect: both are critical training grounds. Parents are preparing young people for the ongoing struggles of human existence. Children tire of hearing the same advice over and over again, but wise parents understand the value of repetition. The important lessons of life need to be constantly reinforced. As a loving parent, the heavenly Father knew there were things His children needed to hear repeatedly for their spiritual safety (Philippians 3:1). These messages were delivered through the preaching and writing of Spirit-guided men like Jude.

REMEMBRANCE AND RIGHTEOUSNESS

Jude wrote to his friends to remind them of things they once knew with certainty but had come to doubt. Most preaching is like that. Sermons seldom provide startling new principles for life. They are, for the most part, reminders to heed what is already known but in danger of being forgotten or neglected.

Why are saved people prone to forget Christ's teaching? Satan uses every resource at his disposal to undermine confidence in God's Word. Secular society is adept at rationalizing its love affair with sin. Worldly-minded people are masterful at making Christians feel intolerant and judgmental for opposing the open practice of immorality.

Some churches even minimize sin. Believers are mentally prepared when the nonreligious reject biblical restraints and scoff at the day of final reckoning, but it is distressing when professed Christians spurn sound doctrine in the name of scholarship or special revelation. If this occurred in Jude's day, why should it be surprising that the trend continues today?

REFORMERS AND RECKLESSNESS

Jude was not ready to concede the church to "reformers" who were nothing more than false teachers in disguise. He believed there were still people who could be counted on to contend for the faith once delivered unto the saints. To encourage his readers to fulfill that mission, he reminded them of the certainty that those who were troubling the church would be punished.

Belief in a day of reckoning has a powerful impact on human be-havior. Paul wrote, "But he who does wrong will be repaid for what he has done, and there is no partiality" (Colossians 3:25). At times, it may appear as if false teachers are succeeding, but God is not finished yet. The disobedient will account for their deeds in due time. Jude used three examples from Israel's history to prove his point: the Israelites who perished in the wilderness, the angels who lost their place in heaven, and the citizens of Sodom who were destroyed by fire. These factual accounts of divine judgment serve as undeniable evidence that God will demand an accounting of the disobedient without regard to their earthly standing.

GOD JUDGES ISRAEL

The Israelites came to dwell in Egypt when Joseph was sold into slavery by his brothers. The Lord overruled their treachery by putting Joseph in a position to save his family from a famine coming upon the entire region. After interpreting Pharaoh's dream foretelling the food shortage, the young Hebrew was placed in charge of storing up rations for the coming crisis. When Jacob sent his sons to find food in Egypt, they were reunited with Joseph, who forgave them and invited them to bring their families to live in the land of Goshen.

The 70 Hebrews who migrated to Egypt became a nation numbering more than a million. The positive political climate eventually changed and the Israelites fell from favor with the government. A king rose to power who was ungrateful for what Joseph had done to help their country survive one of its most desperate hours. The Israelites were enslaved and mistreated, but their cries were heard by God in heaven.

The Lord saved Israel by preparing a deliverer named Moses and empowering him to bring plagues upon Egypt that pressured Pharaoh to let the people go. After releasing the Hebrews, Pharaoh regretted his decision and pursued them with his army. The Lord enabled Moses to part the waters of the Red Sea as an escape route for the Israelites. Far more than a demonstration of divine power, the exodus was an un-mistakable declaration of God's love for His covenant people.

After recalling this history, Jude shifted the attention of his readers to God's wrath, the mysterious side of His love yet an equally perfect part of His nature. The very people He saved from Egypt He later destroyed. How could this be? God's goodness will not keep Him from punishing sin. He will gladly pardon the penitent, but He cannot and will not ignore sin. Because of His holy character, God cannot be indifferent to iniquity.

Jude said that the reason for Israel's destruction was unbelief. The Lord promised to guide the people to a land flowing with milk and honey but warned them He would punish those who refused to keep His covenant. Israel's immorality and idolatry were conclusive evidence that they did not believe God would do what He said. To lose faith is to lose life's most important battle. As John explained, "And this is the victory that has overcome the world – our faith" (1 John 5:4).

Two other New Testament writers made reference to Israel's desert calamity to illustrate the fiasco of faithlessness. The author of Hebrews compared Israel's quest for Canaan to a saint's desire to go to heaven. Like Jude, he saw Israel's failure to occupy the Promised Land as the result of unbelief (Hebrews 3:11, 12, 19–4:2, 11). Christians, like their Old Testament counterparts, must trust God if they are to enter His eternal land of rest.

Paul used Israel's desert debacle to teach the importance of steadfastness (1 Corinthians 10:1-13). The exodus was an impressive beginning for the Jewish nation, yet most of the people never reached their intended destination. The same thing can happen to a Christian (vv. 6-11). Just because a person embarks on a life of faith does not guarantee eternal security in heaven.

God's goodness in saving the Corinthians from their past sins was never intended to suggest that they were privileged pets whose future transgressions would be overlooked. Paul exhorted, "Therefore let him who thinks he stands take heed lest he fall" (1 Corinthians 10:12). What more could possibly be said to awaken slumbering saints from spiritual complacency?

GOD JUDGES ANGELS

Jude's second illustration of the certainty of judgment came from the shocking story of the fallen angels. Apparently these heavenly messengers were dissatisfied with their position as servants of God. Instead of keeping their rightful place of humble submission, they chose to rebel against the Lord's sovereignty. The mutiny against their Maker ended in disaster. Like dishonored angels, people who seem closest to God may actually be farthest from Him in their hearts.

Jude's message is clear: If angels could not avoid punishment for their sins, how much less can mortals hope to escape judgment? God has prepared a place for those who stubbornly resist His will. They will be bound in everlasting chains and held in darkness. It is terrifying to anticipate the future of those who fall into the hands of the living God unprepared for eternity (Hebrews 10:26-31). This is especially true for those who become Christians only to turn their backs on the Lord at some future point (2 Peter 2:20-22).

The day of judgment is approaching. Although false teachers choose to ignore it, they cannot escape it. On that day, all people will appear before the throne of glory to be judged by Christ. The righteous and unrighteous will be separated as a shepherd divides his sheep from the goats. The wicked will hear the pronouncement, "Depart from Me, you cursed, into the everlasting fire prepared for the devil and his angels" (Matthew 25:41). Understanding that defiant men will share the same destiny as obstinate angels, Jude urged his readers to maintain an attitude of loyal, loving obedience to God lest they forfeit their place in heaven.

GOD JUDGES SODOM

Jude's third example of the inevitable punishment for sin centered on the citizens of Sodom and Gomorrah and their neighbors in Admah and Zeboim (Deuteronomy 29:23). This area was the most fertile and well watered in the entire region. Its richness enabled the affluent inhabitants of Sodom to turn to diversions that led to their downfall.

Sexual sins are really symptoms of a far deeper problem: unbelief in God. The "sexual immorality" Jude mentions in verse 7 is a broad term that indicates any type of improper sexual relations. "Strange flesh" refers to physical intimacy with a member of the same sex. Paul denounced homosexuality as a violation of God's will (Romans 1:26-27). The Bible attributes this behavior to spiritual rebellion rather than genetic makeup. When a person will not submit to God, he begins a downward spiral that is observable in the erosion of his standards.

God sent two angels to investigate reports concerning the moral corruption of Sodom. As an important man in that city, Abraham's nephew, Lot, was seated at the city gate and was among the first to greet the angels upon their arrival. Knowing the dangers lurking in Sodom's streets, Lot insisted that they stay at his home for the night.

Before they could retire for the evening, the men of Sodom, young and old alike, surrounded the house. They demanded that Lot hand over his guests so they could molest them. The host pleaded with his neighbors not to violate the sacred protection of his home in order to gratify their wicked desires. Enraged that a relative newcomer had made himself their judge, the Sodomites threatened to do worse things to Lot than what they had planned for his guests.

The men of the city inched forward intending to break down Lot's door. Disaster was averted when the angels struck the men with blindness. The sightless Sodomites wore themselves out while groping to find the entrance. Lot and his daughters fled to the safety of Zoar, and the angels unleashed the fury of heaven upon Sodom and its surrounding cities.

Fire and brimstone rained from the sky and destroyed the cities and their inhabitants. Lot's wife ignored the angel's command not to look back and died as a result of her delay. Her lifeless body became a memorial to the danger of a divided heart.

Jude stated that Sodom and Gomorrah were "set forth" as an example (v. 7). God was making a point in the destruction of these wicked cities, and the Holy Spirit preserved the record to make sure it was never forgotten. To "set forth" means to lie exposed, as a corpse laid out for burial. Like funeral mourners who file by the casket of the deceased, God wanted all humanity to witness the wrath in store for the wicked.

Sodom unmistakably prefigures the suffering to be experienced by the disobedient in the eternal fire of hell. Jesus used Gehenna as a depiction of hell's unending agony. The fires that burned continuously at Jerusalem's trash heap graphically portrayed the eternal torment awaiting sinners. John, whose vivid descriptions of heaven have thrilled saints for centuries, also spoke of a dreaded lake of fire where evil men and women will spend eternity (Revelation 20:15).

On the day of judgment, destruction will come upon the earth as suddenly and unexpectedly as it did for Sodom. It is not possible to pinpoint the exact day and hour of this final reckoning (Luke 17:28-29). What can be known for certain is that sin will be punished (Romans 12:19; 2 Thessalonians 1:8).

DO NOT LOSE HEART

Jude used these stories from Israel's history to remind his readers that God would demand an accounting from the false teachers who were troubling the church. They would not succeed in the end. It is easy to become disheartened when evil appears to be advancing and winning the day, but Christians must not become discouraged and give up their defense of truth. They must never lose confidence that God will punish unrepentant sinners and vindicate the faithful in the end. The last word always belongs to the Lord. Don't you forget it!

DISCUSSION

1. How important is it for Christians to be reminded of fundamentals of the faith?

2. How can Satan make Christians forget or lose confidence in Bible truths? What truths are in danger of being forgotten today?

3. How does belief in final judgment influence human behavior?

4. Why did God punish the Israelites shortly after rescuing them from Egypt?

5. What "domain" or "abode" did the angels of heaven fail to keep?

6. What should Christians learn from God's punishment of the rebellious angels?

7. How does the current moral climate in America compare to that of Sodom and Gomorrah?

8. In speaking of God's judgment on Sodom and Gomorrah, what did Jude mean when he said they were "set forth" as an example?

9. Why did Jude say residents of Sodom and Gomorrah suffered the "vengeance of eternal fire"?

10. Should Christians become disheartened when those who teach religious error appear to go unpunished?

FIVE

The Downfall of Dreamers

Jude 8-10

If I am to know victory, I must fill my heart with holy aspirations.

When people go to war, dreams become their closest traveling companions. Dreams become especially vivid in times of unrest. Some dream of loved ones back home. Others dream of victory and an end to conflict.

BAD DREAMS

Although the word "dream" can be applied to flights of fancy, it is typically used in a more positive sense. Often it refers to making great plans or setting noble goals. It is good to dream boldly for the glory of God and the benefit of His kingdom. Unfortunately, this was not the kind of activity Jude had in mind when he referred to false teachers as "dreamers." Jude wrote about the unholy dreams of wicked men who were attacking the most fundamental beliefs of the church. Whatever he meant by this phrase, it was not intended as a compliment.

Perhaps these men claimed to have received special revelation in the form of dreams that supported their teaching and conduct (Jeremiah

23:25). It is also possible that Jude meant their problems were the result of sinful thoughts that constantly filled their minds. Their thinking was persistently earthly, sensual and devilish (James 3:13-18).

The mindset of these false teachers was reminiscent of man's condition immediately before the flood. Moses wrote, "Then the Lord saw that the wickedness of man was great in the earth, and that every intent of the thoughts of his heart was only evil continually" (Genesis 6:5). Similarly, Paul referred to the ungodly as "inventors of evil things" (Romans 1:30). Sinners often live in a kind of dream world of impurity, totally ignoring the consequences of their actions.

CHARACTERISTICS OF FALSE TEACHERS
• **They Defile the Flesh.** Three charges are leveled against these men as a result of their unholy dreams. First, their immoral thoughts led them to "defile the flesh." In the name of God, and under the supposed protection of His grace, they shamelessly adopted a lifestyle of sin. Those who fill their minds with unwholesome thoughts are inclined to pollute their bodies with unhealthy practices.

No one is immune from the effects of iniquity. Paul declared, "Do not be deceived, God is not mocked; for whatever a man sows, that he will also reap. For he who sows to his flesh will of the flesh reap corruption, but he who sows to the Spirit will of the Spirit reap everlasting life" (Galatians 6:7-8). Christians must not kid themselves about the consequences of sin. God's law of sowing and reaping cannot be circumvented. Disobedience has serious repercussions both in this world and that which is to come.

Defilement is the only possible outcome when a person caters to the cravings of his lower nature. Sowing to the flesh degrades the body, corrupts the character, and stains the soul. Christians must make it their aim to glorify God rather than gratify the flesh (1 Corinthians 6:19-20). With the help of the Spirit, evil lusts can be subdued (Galatians 5:16-18; Romans 8:13; Genesis 4:7).

Paul commanded Christians to present their bodies as a living sacrifice to God (Romans 12:1). This offering involves a spiritual transformation accomplished through the renewing of the mind (v. 2). Good lives are the product of good thoughts. Conversely, evil lives are the product of evil thoughts. Defilement can always be traced back to the unholy thinking from which it originated.

• **They Reject Authority.** Jude's second indictment against these "filthy dreamers" (v. 8 KJV) was that they "reject authority." God has established a system of authority in this world to restrain people from carrying out improper thoughts and desires. These restraints are rejected by the ungodly because they interfere with the fulfillment of their plans.

Consider the home. Children are blessed with parents as their earliest authority figures. Young people are instructed to honor and obey their moms and dads because it is right (Ephesians 6:1). God knew that adults have the knowledge and wisdom necessary to safely guide less experienced adolescents through the turbulent teen years. Children who heed their parents' advice can expect to live longer, happier lives as a result.

Yet parental authority will occasionally be rejected by young people. Parents must be careful not to provoke their children to wrath, but even good parents may find their son or daughter out of control. Some disagreement is normal, but friction is usually kept in check by a relationship of mutual love. When unholy thoughts are left unrestrained, they will eventually override the natural affection that bonds family members together (Romans 1:30-31). At that point, outright rebellion may be declared.

Civil authority is another of God's blessings. It is specially designed to curb sinfulness in society where it takes the form of crime. In Romans 13:1-7, Paul declared that government is God-ordained and rulers are His ministers. Their purpose is to encourage good and to execute wrath upon evildoers.

People should subject themselves to higher powers not only to avoid punishment, but also because their consciences tell them it is the proper thing to do. External restraints are only necessary for those who reject the internal restraint provided by God. Even if there were no police officers, courts or jails, the law should still be obeyed for conscience's sake. When impure thoughts are left unbridled, they can sear the conscience until it is of no effect. At that point, laws that interfere with satisfying the flesh are easily disregarded.

In addition to providing authority for families and communities, God has blessed Christians with authority in the church. Elders are the divinely appointed overseers of local congregations (Acts 14:23; 20:28). The Hebrews writer commanded, "Obey those who rule over you, and be submissive, for they watch out for your souls, as those who must give account. Let them do so with joy and not with grief, for that would be unprofitable for you" (Hebrews 13:17).

The restraints God placed in the home, society and local church are there to promote a holy life. When they are ignored, the only possible outcome is moral and spiritual decline. Those who lack proper respect for authority figures (domestic, civil, spiritual or divine) will suffer because of their headstrong ways.

• **They Speak Evil of Dignitaries.** The third charge brought against these false teachers was that they "speak evil of dignitaries." Dignitaries are persons (heavenly or earthly) who deserve to be highly regarded because of their station. It is not uncommon for the ungodly to speak contemptuously of leaders who resist their worldliness.

Jude's interest was in the archangel's attitude during this anxious episode. Michael refused to engage in "reviling accusations" against his opponent. He would not allow the confrontation to degenerate into an unrestrained battle of emotions.

The way Michael, the archangel, conducted himself when contending with the devil stood in stark contrast to the disrespectful treatment false teachers were giving godly leaders in the church (Jude 9). Michael was engaged in a dispute with the devil about the body of Moses. After Moses glimpsed the Promised Land from the heights of Pisgah, he died and was buried by the Lord in a Moabite valley (Deuteronomy 34:6). When Satan attempted to interfere, he was confronted by this distinguished member of the heavenly host. No matter how just the cause or evil the opponent, one must be careful not to be led into sinful speech. It is possible to be right and still be wrong.

Reviling accusations are harsh terms of reproach. As tension escalates, it is common for conversations to become increasingly personal and cruel. When it became clear to Michael that Satan could not be reasoned with, he wisely brought the dispute to a conclusion by saying, "The Lord rebuke you." When obstinate people are determined to do wrong, there comes a time to leave the matter in God's hands.

Christians can learn a valuable lesson from this incident. How does a child of God deal with unpleasant and contentious people? Even when a person is confident he is right, it is not wise to enter into a war of words that can lead to sin. This does not mean it is inappropriate to discuss religion or dispute false doctrine. The key is for children of God to conduct themselves in the highest manner at all times.

When serious differences make emotions run high, the greatest caution must be exercised. One of Satan's favorite snares is to trap those defending truth with their own tongue. If the greatest of all good angels guarded his speech when contending with the most evil of all fallen angels, then how ought men to conduct themselves when contending for the faith? Even righteous indignation must be controlled or it can deteriorate into raw anger and hatred.

AWESOME INTELLECTS OR ANIMAL IMPULSES

The false teachers Jude confronted rushed in where angels dared not tread. Unlike Michael, they did not hesitate to speak evil of opponents who were far more righteous than they. They justified their ruthless words and condescending tone by claiming to possess a higher knowledge of God's will.

Despite their bold assertions, they were completely out of touch with God's Word (1 Corinthians 2:14). The only special knowledge they possessed was of base things. Instead of great thinkers, they were like unreasoning animals. Jude called them "brute beasts" (v. 10) implying they had sunk to the level of creatures that live by instinct. Their confused state of mind led them to corrupt their bodies with harmful practices.

Because man is created in the image of God, he is above the animals. Human beings have the unique capacity to reason. They can know right from wrong and have the ability to choose between the two. Christians have a special incentive to choose carefully because their bodies are the temple of the Holy Spirit (1 Corinthians 6:19).

People whose lives are dominated by sin mentally inhabit a dream-like world of impurity. Over time, they become proficient at justifying their reckless behavior in the name of spiritual or intellectual enlightenment. TV shows, popular music and movies often glorify an animal-like existence. Sadly, religious leaders can also be found to rationalize almost any sin.

RULES FOR RIGHTEOUS LIVING

In view of man's higher nature, Jude provided three principles for proper Christian conduct. First, saints should keep their bodies and minds pure from those things that defile them. Second, they must show proper respect for rightful authority. Third, even when contending for the faith, Christians must speak the truth in love. God's patriots must fill their hearts with holy aspirations. Those who do will enjoy the sweet dreams of a clear conscience.

DISCUSSION

1. How can the word "dream" be used in a positive sense?

2. What did Jude mean by the expression "dreamers"?

3. What three charges does Jude level against these dreamers?

4. How is defiling the flesh an outgrowth of one's dreams?

5. What does it mean to "reject authority"?

6. How does God restrain people from carrying out sinful thoughts and desires?

7. What is the response of immoral men and women to those who resist the open practice of their sins?

8. What can Christians learn from Michael about dealing with difficult people?

9. Why does Jude liken false teachers to "brute beasts"?

10. How can Christians maintain a Christlike demeanor while contending for the faith?

SIX

A Road Less Traveled

Jude 11a

If I am to know victory, I must choose my path carefully.

During times of war, retreating forces will often swap road signs indicating the names of streets or the direction of particular cities. The aim is to confuse the enemy and slow his advance. With a good map and compass, it is easy to sort things out and identify the correct route. Careless travelers, however, can be led astray by their inattention.

WOE MEANS WHOA

Satan delights in luring unsuspecting souls down avenues leading away from God. That is why Jude alerted His readers to beware of the devil's tactics. Christians must choose carefully which road they will travel in life. To seize their attention and help them comprehend the peril of picking the wrong path, Jude began his admonition with the word, "Woe."

"Woe" is an arresting, heart-stopping word. Jesus used it to rebuke the privileged cities of Chorazin, Bethsaida and Capernaum (Matthew

11:21-24). They were blessed by His presence and witnessed His mighty works, yet they refused to repent. He added that it would be more tolerable for the city of Sodom in the judgment than for these citizens who neglected their unique opportunities.

"Woe" envisions the future outpouring of God's wrath on those who live unrighteously. It is a reproach, a warning and a guarantee all rolled into one. It says that unless one's course is altered, the consequences will be devastating. Jude applied this word to men who were teaching false doctrine and troubling the church.

The reason for this strong language was that these men were traveling the same crooked course as three of the most notorious characters in all the divine record. The false teachers were matching footprints with Cain, Balaam and Korah along their downward paths. Jude used this trio as an example of what not to be and exhorted his readers to choose a higher road in life.

This lesson will focus on what Jude called "the way of Cain." The term "way" is often used in Scripture to refer to the course of a person's life. Human beings are free to choose the path they will travel and ought to do so carefully. Cain chose the wrong road and paid a dear price. Jude was marking Cain's path with warning signs so no one would wander it by mistake.

SELF-WILL

Cain was the older of two sons born into earth's first family. His brother, Abel, loved animals and chose shepherding as his life's occupation. Cain followed in the steps of his father and became a farmer (Genesis 4:2; 2:15).

The way of Cain first came to light when he and his brother were making offerings to God (Genesis 4:1-5). Abel sacrificed the best of his flock, and the Lord received his gift with favor. Cain brought some produce he had grown, but God would not accept it. The difference between the two offerings was noted in the epistle to the Hebrews: "By faith Abel offered to God a more excellent sacrifice than Cain, through which he obtained witness that he was righteous, God testifying of his gifts; and through it he being dead still speaks" (Hebrews 11:4).

The excellence of Abel's sacrifice was that it was offered by faith.

According to Romans 10:17, faith comes by hearing and hearing by the word of God. Having heard God's directions, Abel did not stray from them.

It is difficult to imagine that Abel acted without divine direction and spontaneously chose to honor the Lord by making a blood sacrifice of one of his precious lambs. Was it mere coincidence that his choice of a gift prefigured the sacrificial system of the Levitical priesthood and the offering of Jesus, the Lamb of God who takes away the sins of the world? It is more reasonable to believe that he acted at the command of God and was commended for closely observing the Lord's instructions while Cain followed them more loosely and was reprimanded.

Cain may have felt that his produce was better than the bloody sacrifice of Abel's smelly sheep. It is possible that he was seeking to impress God by trying to improve on the divine command. Regardless of the intent, it was an act of disobedience. As Samuel told Saul, "To obey is better than sacrifice" (1 Samuel 15:22). *Whenever a man substitutes his own will for that of God's, he is following the way of Cain.*

There is little doubt that Cain's sin commenced with an improper disposition, but the result was a disobedient act. God's acceptance of Abel's offering attested to his righteousness. John stated, "He who practices righteousness is righteous" (1 John 3:7). By failing to do what God commanded, Cain showed himself to be unrighteous.

SULLENNESS

Cain was upset that God rejected his offering, and his downcast face revealed his bitterness. Paul provided excellent counsel for a person in Cain's state of mind: "Be angry, and do not sin: do not let the sun go down on your wrath" (Ephesians 4:26). Christians must learn to manage their emotions by channeling pent-up energy toward constructive ends. Cain was unwilling to let go of his resentment and allowed his anger to control him. *Those who live at the mercy of their emotions are traveling the path of Cain.*

The Lord attempted to reason with Cain but to no avail. He asked the young man to consider why he was upset. Certainly he was disappointed, but why blame his brother? If he was upset with anyone, it ought to have been himself. *Those who blame others for their problems are following the way of Cain.*

God encouraged Cain to change his course while there was still time. If he would start doing what was right, he would still be accepted. If not, sin was ready to pounce on him like a hungry lion stalking its prey. Sin would always be present, but he had the power to resist it. That fact remains true in the Christian age. Paul assured the Corinthians that there is always a way of escape from temptation (1 Corinthians 10:13). *That means that those who follow in Cain's way do so by choice.*

Instead of listening to God's advice, Cain clung to his anger until it vented itself in murder. Whatever a person fills his heart with will eventually find a way to express itself. Couples who are in love constantly look for ways to bring happiness to each other. People who harbor grudges are like walking time bombs waiting to detonate. Sometimes that negative energy is released inwardly in the form of ulcers, stroke or heart attack. Other times it will erupt outwardly in hurtful speech or physical violence. In either case, anger harms the one in whom it dwells more than the one toward whom it is directed.

SELFISHNESS

Cain lured his brother to a secluded field and killed him. At that moment, he took his own life as well. Whenever a person hates his fellow man, he abides in spiritual death (1 John 3:14). John used the sad story of Cain and Abel to exhort Christians to choose a different course in their own personal relationships: "For this is the message that you heard from the beginning, that we should love one another, not as Cain who was of the wicked one and murdered his brother. And why did he murder him? Because his works were evil and his brother's righteous" (1 John 3:11-12).

It is intriguing to observe the connection between Cain's attitude toward God and his actions toward Abel. The two were inseparably linked. If he would substitute his will for God's in worship, he would not hesitate to elevate his will over that of his brother. *Cain's way is the way of selfishness*, and those who are closest to one who is traveling this road should beware. Friendships, marriages and relationships of every description have been callously destroyed as a result of consuming self-interest.

Although fully aware of what transpired, the Lord confronted Cain with a question to make him stop and think about his actions: "Where is Abel your brother?" (Genesis 4:9). Cain coldly responded, "I do not know. Am I my brother's keeper?" His cool, uncaring attitude revealed the reason for his predicament. Where love is lacking, trouble is soon to follow. The golden rule is displaced by the law of the jungle.

When Christians come to a fork in the road of any relationship, Paul urged them to choose the more excellent way of love (1 Corinthians 12:31–13:13). The most loving path is always the one that follows Christ's teaching. In his epistle to the Romans, Paul expounded on the need for enduring love in human relationships:

> Owe no one anything except to love one another, for he who loves another has fulfilled the law. For the commandments, "You shall not commit adultery," "You shall not murder," "You shall not steal," "You shall not bear false witness," "You shall not covet," and if there is any other commandment, are all summed up in this saying, namely, "You shall love your neighbor as yourself." Love does no harm to a neighbor; therefore love is the fulfillment of the law. (Romans 13:8-10)

SELF-DECEIT

It was also Cain's way to lie about his sin. Rather than face his guilt, he attempted to cover it up the same way he must have hidden his brother's body. For a fleeting moment, he thought he might not be discovered, but that was not to be the case. God told Cain that Abel's blood cried out from the ground demanding justice. As a result of his sin, he could no longer pursue the occupation he loved. Rather than living the settled life of a farmer, he would spend his days as a wandering fugitive.

God remembered mercy, however, and placed a mark upon Cain as a warning not to kill him. Yet, the consequences of Cain's sin were almost unbearable. He had to live with the knowledge that he had murdered his brother, broken his parents' hearts, and inflicted a terrible burden on his future family. The tentacles of sin touched the lives of all who loved him.

Jude declared that false teachers are going the way of Cain. They are his spiritual descendants because they prefer their own way to that of God. They are selfish and sensual and quick to vent their anger on anyone who opposes them. They defy God while constantly denying any wrongdoing. In the end, those who choose to walk in the way of Cain must also share in his punishment.

WEIGH YOUR WAY

Every person must choose a path to travel in life. Jesus narrowed the choice to one of two ways (Matthew 7:13-14). One is broad, undemanding and crowded with fun-loving companions. The other is narrow, difficult and sometimes lonely.

When standing at the crossroads, the natural choice seems to be the wide road. At journey's end, one gains a whole new perspective. People who have traveled this spacious street seem surprised to find that its destination is utter devastation (Matthew 7:22-23). Ruin waits patiently at the end of the path of least resistance, and those who fail to think ahead will be greeted one day by misery. Yet those who take this wrong turn on life's road can blame no one but themselves because Jesus and Jude have clearly marked the way.

The prophets have always encouraged people to make a wise choice of the road they will travel in life. Samuel announced, "I will teach you the good and the right way" (1 Samuel 12:23). Jeremiah pleaded, "Stand in the ways and see, And ask for the old paths, where the good way is, And walk in it; Then you will find rest for your souls" (Jeremiah 6:16). The right way has always been lit by God's Word. The psalmist proclaimed, "Through your precepts I get understanding: therefore I hate every false way. Your word is a lamp to my feet and a light to my path" (Psalm 119:104-105).

In the highest sense, Christ is the way to heaven. On the eve of His death, Jesus declared, "I am the way, the truth, and the life. No one comes to the Father except through Me" (John 14:6). By virtue of His death upon the cross, He opened up a new and living way to the presence of God (Hebrews 9:8; 10:20). That is why Christianity, in its earliest days, actually became known as "the way" (Acts 19:9, 23; 24:14). Those who reject Christ will find no alternate route leading to glory (4:12; Hebrews 2:3; 10:26-29). Only dead ends and disappointment await.

What path are you traveling today? Is it the way of Cain, paved with selfishness, presumption, hatred, lies and wrath? Or is it the way of Christ, marked by humility, love, obedience, honesty and grace? God's patriots must be determined to follow Jesus no matter how difficult the journey. If you do not like the direction you are headed, it is not too late to change course. God has provided you with a free will and a conscience to guide it. Each person must ultimately decide his own destiny. In the final analysis, it is a choice between life and death (Jeremiah 21:8). Which path will you choose?

DISCUSSION

1. What does the word "woe" mean?

2. Name three notorious characters to whom Jude compared false teachers.

3. How is life like a pathway?

4. When did Cain's evil way first come to light?

5. How were the false teachers following the way of Cain?

6. Why is love called a more excellent way?

7. How does God's Word light man's path?

8. What did Jesus mean when He said, "I am the way"?

9. Why were early Christians referred to as those of "the way"?

10. What does Jude's warning against following the way of Cain say about man's free will?

SEVEN

In Hot Pursuit!

Jude 11a, b

If I am to know victory, I must make pleasing God my highest aim.

Why does a person enter military service? Some want to travel and see the world. Others are thrill seekers who find the adventure (and danger) exhilarating. Quite a few choose a career in the service for financial rewards (college tuition, home loans, medical coverage and early retirement).

Then there are the patriots: farmers, teachers, factory workers and businessmen who are not career soldiers, yet these honorable citizens can be counted on in a time of crisis. These are men and women who serve their country out of loyalty rather than personal gain. They enlist, not because they love a good fight, but because they believe in defending what is right! They are peacemakers, not pleasure seekers or profiteers.

Similarly, God's patriots are people with high spiritual aims. They are ordinary Christians who are reluctant to fight yet prepared to stand and be counted for truth when duty demands it. To the contrary, false teachers are motivated by things like notoriety, paychecks, selfish agendas or the intoxicating smell of battle. The prophet Balaam was just such a man.

A PRAYER WORTH PURSUING

From the lofty heights overlooking the plains of Moab, amid the sweet smell of sacrifice to the Most High God, came one of the most beautiful prayers ever prayed. Couched in that prayer was a phrase expressing the supreme purpose of life: "Let me die the death of the righteous" (Numbers 23:10). These words spoken by the prophet Balaam challenge those who read them to pursue this worthwhile goal. Unfortunately, the prophet did not heed his own plea.

Every intelligent man and woman realizes that death is certain. The only thing that matters is whether one is counted among the righteous at that time. Earthly standing will be of no consequence when appearing before the throne of God. Prosperity, power and popularity are worldly vanities that pale in the presence of One who is no respecter of persons.

On one hand, the word "righteous" describes how an individual should treat his fellow man. Honesty and fairness are at the heart of this virtue. In a higher sense, Christians recognize that righteousness refers to a person's standing before God. The gospel is heaven's plan for making imperfect people right with the Lord through the death of Christ upon the cross.

The importance of righteousness is stressed throughout the pages of Scripture. But for 10 such men, Sodom might still stand today (Genesis 18:23-32). If only one good man had been found in Jerusalem, Jeremiah said that God would have spared the city from destruction at the hands of Nebuchadnezzar (Jeremiah 5:1). On Earth's last day, the angels will search the planet for righteous men and women who will "shine forth as the sun in the kingdom of their Father" (Matthew 13:41-43).

THE CURSE OF COVETOUSNESS

Balaam's desire to meet death in a right relationship with God was admirable, yet his life did not measure up to his prayer. Although he wanted to please God, he wanted the wealth of this world even more. When these desires came into conflict, the prophet's actions revealed what mattered most in his life.

Jude saw the error of Balaam repeating itself in the church (Jude 11). Religious leaders who gave the appearance of being righteous were actually preoccupied with earthly concerns. Greed caused them to put the flesh before the Spirit.

Covetousness is a subtle sin that is difficult to perceive at the start. In time, those who blind themselves to their materialism will not only defend their actions but also run unrestrained after more possessions. It led Judah to sell his brother and Judas his Savior. In actuality, a man who succumbs to greed has sold his own soul.

Love of money is unquestionably the root of all kinds of evil (1 Timothy 6:10). Those who chase wealth are more likely to find sorrow than satisfaction. How many people have been seduced by earthly riches and betrayed the faith they love?

The apostle Paul offered an excellent alternative to the headlong pursuit of worldly gain. He encouraged Christians to pursue righteousness (1 Timothy 6:11) and trust in the Lord to supply their needs (v. 17). Their craving should be for spiritual wealth measured in good works laid up against the day of judgment. Eternal life awaits those who set the affection of their hearts on things above (Colossians 3:2).

To fully appreciate Jude's warning, it is important to recall the events surrounding Balaam's life. The temptation to repeat his error is ever-present, as it was with the false teachers Jude confronted in the first century. Christians must resist covetousness at all costs.

FIRST IMPRESSIONS ARE DECEIVING

When Balaam was first introduced in Scripture, it seems that his desire to live a righteous life was genuine. Somewhere along the way, that changed. Gradually, almost imperceptibly, he shifted the focus of his life from serving God to satisfying himself.

Having escaped bondage in Egypt, the Israelites arrived at the Plains of Moab while en route to the Promised Land. Balak, the King of Moab, was troubled by their presence after hearing of Israel's victories over Sihon and Og. It had not been long since Sihon defeated the Moabite army in battle; now there was one even more powerful with whom to contend.

At wit's end, Balak sent a message to Balaam asking for help against the interlopers (Numbers 22:5-6). Apparently Balaam had quite a reputation for successfully predicting the outcome of battles. Whomever he cursed was cursed, and whomever he blessed was blessed. As a side note, it is interesting to observe that God did not leave Himself without witness in nations other than Israel: there was Melchizedek in pre-Israelite Canaan, Naaman's servant in Syria, Jeremiah in Egypt, Jonah in Assyria, and Balaam in Moab.

Initially, Balaam makes a favorable impression upon those who read his life's story. He was clearly a religious man with a unique relationship to God. After hearing the Moabite king's request for help, he consulted God before giving his reply. That night, the Lord spoke to Balaam and revealed that the Israelites were His chosen people. Balaam relayed God's message to his visitors the next morning. They were disappointed to hear that he was denied permission to go with them.

By passing up the opportunity to become personally wealthy, Balaam gave every indication of being an obedient servant of the Lord. Regrettably, things are not always what they seem. In the face of intensified temptation, the character of Balaam began to unravel.

THE SIN OF THE SECOND LOOK

The elders from Moab returned home and told their King that Balaam refused to come with them. Yet something in his reply convinced Balak that he should not give up. Balaam left the impression that he would gladly have accepted the offer if the Lord had given His approval. How different things might have been if he had said, "I refuse to go with you!"

The Lord is not pleased with disgruntled servants who reluctantly do His will. John wrote, "For this is the love of God, that we keep His commandments. And His commandments are not burdensome" (1 John 5:3). Christians should be eager, willing servants who carry out God's commands cheerfully.

Despite Balaam's refusal, Balak was intent on securing his assistance. He probably thought the prophet was playing hard-to-get in hopes of obtaining a higher fee for his services. This time, the King sent a larger and more distinguished group of dignitaries to negotiate the deal. They carried with them promises of greater riches if Balaam would accompany them back to their country and place a curse upon their enemy.

Like Balak, Satan does not give up easily. He is convinced that every person can be bought for a price. If one temptation does not work, he simply returns at a later time with a more enticing offer.

Jesus raised a thought-provoking question to strengthen His disciples' resistance to covetousness. He asked, "For what profit is it to a man if he gains the whole world, and loses his own soul? Or what will a man give in exchange for his soul?" (Matthew 16:26). No temporary pleasure or momentary possession can ever make up for the loss of personal integrity or eternal security.

When the ambassadors arrived with their new proposal, Balaam's response was impressive. He told them that if Balak offered him his palace filled with gold and silver, he could not go beyond the word of the Lord to do more or less. Nevertheless, he asked the emissaries to spend the night while he consulted with God a second time to see if He had changed His mind concerning this matter.

Sadly, Balaam had not accepted God's will. He should have told his guests that God had already spoken and the matter was settled. Instead, greed led him to pursue the Moabites' wealth rather than his Master's will. It is never enough to inquire of God's will. One must ask with the right attitude (James 4:3).

Sometimes the worst punishment God can inflict is to let a person have his own way. When a man is determined to pursue sin, God will reluctantly give him up to his desires (Romans 1:24, 26, 28). Such was the case with Balaam. The Lord allowed him to undertake the trip to Moab on the condition that he speak only those words revealed to him from heaven. God told Balaam he *could* go, but He never said he *should* go. There is a profound difference between permission and approval.

Taking a second look at sin cannot make it less sinful. All it does is make the beholder more tolerant of sin. If a person's heart is not pure, it is possible to rationalize and condone almost any course of action.

It is not hard to imagine Balaam's excitement as he undertook what he hoped to be a very profitable trip. He set out by donkey to his destination. Things went well at first, but that was soon to change.

DELIBERATIONS WITH A DONKEY

For no apparent reason, the donkey veered off the road into a field. The prophet wrestled with the reins, struck the beast, and was able to steer her back onto the path. A short time later, he came to a place where the road was hemmed in by two walls that protected vineyards. The donkey thrust herself against one of the walls and crushed her rider's foot. Once again, Balaam angrily struck his mount. Further down the road, they came to a narrow place with barely enough room to get through. This time, the donkey sat down and refused to take another step.

Enraged, Balaam beat the animal mercilessly with his staff. As he vented his fury, the donkey cried out, "What have I done to you, that you have struck me these three times?" (Numbers 22:28). Without realizing the absurdity of talking to an animal, Balaam replied that she was making him look foolish. He added that if a sword had been available, he would have killed her on the spot.

The donkey asked the prophet if he had noticed that her actions were out of character. The implication was that he should have realized there was a reason for her unusual behavior. Balaam acknowledged that her escapades that day were not typical of her past performance. As he spoke, the Lord opened his eyes and allowed him to see an angel with sword in hand standing in the narrow spot of the road.

WORLDLY AND GODLY SORROW

The angel took up questioning where the donkey left off. Balaam was asked why he was beating this creature that had just saved his life. The reason for the animal's strange behavior was that she saw the messenger of God standing in the road three different times. She was in no danger, but Balaam would surely have been slain had she not taken evasive steps. God was angry with Balaam, and the angel had come to confront him because of his headlong pursuit of wealth.

To his credit, Balaam confessed his sin. To his shame, he did not truly repent. The prophet told the angel that if continuing the trip displeased him, he would go home at once. If? Was it really necessary to ask? God told him not to take the trip in the first place. Now it nearly cost him his life. How different things could have been had he returned home immediately.

Paul must have been thinking of someone like Balaam when he wrote about the difference between worldly and godly sorrow (2 Corinthians 7:10). Sorrow that does not lead to personal change is worthless. How many modern Balaams continue recklessly down the road of disobedience despite repeated warnings to turn back? Self-restraint is essential for anyone who would die the death of the righteous.

Peter said it was love for the wages of unrighteousness that lay behind the prophet's determined journey (2 Peter 2:15). He used his position and influence to enrich himself at the expense of God's people. When teachers are more interested in money and acclaim than truth and faithfulness, they are repeating Balaam's error. It is no surprise, then, that many church problems come from large, affluent congregations and from popular preachers who gain notoriety through writing and speaking (2 Timothy 4:3).

The incentive for compromise is like the constant pull of gravity: ever present yet out of mind. It is doubtful that Balaam admitted his true motives to himself. Likewise, false teachers attribute their antics to noble intentions and deny any responsibility for the spiritual and relational carnage left in their wake.

THE TABLE IS TURNED

The angel allowed Balaam to continue his inadvisable course with one stipulation: that he speak only what God would tell him. Finally, the prophet reached his destination and was greeted by the Moabite king. Balaam was quick to explain that he could only speak the words given to him by God. Under the protection of this disclaimer, Balaam looked forward to the next day when he hoped to become a wealthy man.

The following morning, Balak took Balaam to one of the high places of Baal. From that consecrated site, he could see the Israelites stretched out across the plain as far as the eye could see. He commenced to construct seven altars and sacrificed seven bulls and seven rams in an effort to appease God's wrath and seek His favor.

Balaam's attempt to substitute ceremony for decency is still a common practice. Many who spend their week in a headlong pursuit of wealth or pleasure will pray on Sundays for God to forgive their unscrupulous conduct and spiritual neglect. Just as the Lord rejected Balaam's offering, He will spurn the empty prayers of those who think they can exchange a religious act for a holy life.

Balaam made four attempts to curse the chosen people of God. Each time he failed miserably. Instead of a curse, a blessing proceeded from his lips. With every try, the blessing became even stronger.

The account of Balaam's reversal became one of Israel's favorite stories as time passed. Moses (Deuteronomy 23:4), Joshua (Joshua 24:9), Nehemiah (Nehemiah 13:2), and Micah (Micah 6:5) all appealed to this historic event as evidence of God's ability to turn the table on those who would harm His people. The apostle Paul provided Christians with similar assurance: "And we know that all things work together for good to those who love God, to those who are the called according to His purpose" (Romans 8:28).

PULLING OUT ALL THE STOPS

Balak was disappointed that the prophet was unable to curse his enemies, but he was outraged that he had blessed them. He refused to pay Balaam, who must have sensed that his life was now in danger. In a final desperate move, the prophet succeeded in bringing a curse upon the Israelites. Balaam realized that as long as Israel obeyed God, they could not be hurt. The key was to separate them from their Protector. If they could be enticed to sin against the Lord, then the consequence would be more disastrous than any curse he could pronounce upon them.

It was a brilliant strategy, but how could he induce the Israelites to sin? Balaam decided to use the Moabite women to lead Israel astray. Balak adopted his advice and a once-holy nation soon found itself immersed in adultery and idolatry. Balaam's tactic has been used successfully on endless occasions since that time (Revelation 2:14). That is why the Bible repeatedly warns God's people against uniting themselves unequally with unbelievers (2 Corinthians 6:14). Religious error and immorality are natural consequences of establishing strong ties with those outside the family of God. Christians should love all people, but the most intimate relationships of life are best reserved for those within the covenant community.

It is sad to see the depths to which Balaam had sunk. His selfishness became so severe that he lost all concern for anyone but himself. A terrible plague broke out among the Israelites, claiming 24,000 lives. The outbreak was halted when Phinehas, son of the high priest, atoned for the people's sins by executing one of the most brazen offenders who brought a Midianite woman into the midst of the camp (Numbers 25:7).

Although Balaam thought he succeeded, he was badly mistaken. His selfishness had merely sealed his own doom. In one of the four oracles he delivered from the high places of Baal, he had spoken those memorable words, "Let me die the death of the righteous." After a later battle with Israel, his body was found among the corpses of the slain idolaters (Numbers 31:8). To die as the righteous, one must live righteously.

RELISHING RIGHTEOUSNESS

It is not enough to know God's will; a person must cherish it (2 Thessalonians 2:11-12). The righteous are people who not only sorrow over sin but turn from it also. They pursue eternal blessings rather than momentary pleasures. Holy people sacrifice their hearts to God and nothing less. They seek the welfare of their fellow man and the good of the church above their own narrow interests.

God's patriots have the hearts of fighters, but their motivation is different from ruthless mercenaries such as Balaam. Their actions are guided by love and principle rather than by lust and greed. They have a higher cause and are guided by a nobler ethic. Jude's warning against running greedily after the error of Balaam is still needed in the church today. Every man and every woman is after something in this life. What will you choose to pursue?

DISCUSSION

1. Why should one's goals be evaluated in light of the certainty of death?

2. Define the term "righteousness."

3. How can a person die the death of the righteous?

4. When a person's words and actions clash, which is more believable?

5. Why is sorrow over sin insufficient to secure salvation?

6. Are all people after something in life? What are you pursuing?

7. Does Satan give up easily when resisted?

EIGHT

A Season of Discontent

Jude 11a, c

---

*If I am to know victory, I must be content
without becoming complacent.*

Many men are eager to volunteer for battle, but few are prepared to endure military life without complaint. They enlist in a heat of passion, and sometime later reality begins to set in. When hardship becomes a way of life, it is easy to become disgruntled. Those in positions of authority may be viewed as the enemy, instead of the original foe.

The winter spent in Valley Forge caused many soldiers to question the leadership of Gen. George Washington. Dissatisfaction was rampant among Sam Houston's men as they continually retreated from the Mexican Army led by Santa Anna. In the end, patience was vindicated as Americans and Texans won their freedom. Victory over sin equally depends on steady submission to divinely appointed authority.

The devil is delighted when discontented Christians engage in acts of spiritual insubordination. God's patriots must refuse to cast their lot with insurgents who would divide the people of God. A time comes when conscientious Christians must go their separate ways, but parting should be tearful, not prideful. An unchristlike spirit is nearly always at the heart of church splits.

CONFRONTING SPIRITUAL INSURGENCY

Jude's readers were deeply disturbed by an insurrection occurring in their home congregation. False teachers were leading a revolt against godly leaders in the church. To aid his friends in their hour of crisis, Jude pointed them to the example of Moses who successfully withstood a group of rebels attempting to divide and conquer the nation of Israel.

During 40 years of wilderness wandering, many events distressed Moses. Once his own brother and sister jealously tried to seize control of the nation. At Marah an uprising was sparked by a water shortage. While camped at Kadesh-barnea, Israel refused to undertake the conquest of Canaan when God commanded it.

Of all the opposition Moses faced, however, the most formidable was a rebellion led by a man named Korah. This uprising was not the impulsive revolt of a few discouraged people. It was not the insurrection of a confused crowd without any definite aims. Korah's rebellion was an organized conspiracy with a capable man at the head of it.

Something about the false teachers Jude was confronting reminded him of this Old Testament character and the ugly episode that resulted from his selfish motives. "Woe to them! For they have ... perished in the rebellion of Korah" (Jude 11). Jude accomplished two things when he penned these words. First, he rebuked those who oppose godly men in places of divinely appointed authority. Second, he applauded Moses as an example of how to deal effectively with divisive, disgruntled people.

OPPORTUNISTS AND INSURRECTION

The soul of the mutiny was Korah, who was a Levite but not a priest. He was consumed with envy because the latter position was given exclusively to the sons of Aaron. Dathan, Abiram and On were also ringleaders of the rebellion. As descendants of Reuben, the oldest son of Jacob, they probably had trouble accepting the fact that offspring of Reuben's younger brother Levi were in a position of leadership over them. They must have felt they had lost their rightful place of prestige as progeny of Israel's firstborn son.

Joining them were 250 princes of Israel. These men were not mere rabble but chief men of the congregation. They were well-known, highly respected individuals whose opinions were influential with the population at large. Perhaps their bitterness was the result of being overlooked when Moses appointed 70 men to serve as judges to assist him in governing.

Regardless of their motives, these political opportunists knew the time was ripe for rebellion. Israel had been soundly defeated by the Canaanites at Kadesh-barnea. Following on the heels of this embarrassing reversal was Moses' announcement that they would spend the next 40 years living in the wilderness as a result of their disobedience.

The news must have sounded like a death sentence, especially to older members of the nation. No longer did they dream of a homeland in Canaan. In fact, the quicker they could get out of that desert and return to Egypt, the better off they thought they would be.

Rather than accepting personal responsibility for their predicament, they laid the blame at the feet of Moses and Aaron. The charge brought against Moses was that he had gone too far. They accused him of usurping his authority as leader of the nation. In their minds, he was nothing more than a self-appointed dictator.

The rebels twisted God's words to defend their insurgency. To give the revolt some semblance of legitimacy, they misapplied God's declaration that Israel was a kingdom of priests and that all of its citizens were holy (Exodus 19:6). The statement was true, but the inference they drew from it was not. Every Israelite was special to God, but it was wrong to conclude that He had no special roles for select groups or individuals.

HANDLING PERSONAL ATTACKS

Moses never shone more brightly than on this occasion. His handling of the crisis serves as a model for those who find themselves misunderstood and maligned by others. The first thing he did was carry his burden to God in prayer. He must have been heartbroken by the seething accusations directed against him. At this point, it would have been easy to give up in disgust or strike back in anger, but Moses laid his troubles and his temper at the feet of God.

To his critics, Moses proposed a test. Offering incense was one of the highest duties of priests. If these rebels wanted the priesthood so badly, then let them come before the tabernacle of the Lord with censers in hand, and let God choose between them and the sons of Aaron.

The proposal was particularly sobering in light of what had happened to Nadab and Abihu a short time earlier (Leviticus 10:1-3). While offering incense to God they were consumed by fire. The Lord explained that their punishment was the result of ignoring His instructions regarding the type of fire to be used in this act of worship. Could a similar fate be waiting those who disregarded His authority concerning who was to make such an offering?

Moses cast the accusation of his adversaries back at them. He told them they were the ones who had gone too far! Those who create division by rejecting rightful authority have definitely stepped beyond the boundaries of God's will.

In standing against Moses and Aaron, Korah and his henchmen were actually rebelling against God! The miracles performed by Moses and Aaron were unmistakable proof of God's backing. If the Lord had appointed these men to lead the nation, then to reject them was tantamount to rejecting Him. What Korah really wanted was absolute freedom to do as he pleased. His defense of the revolt was a matter of public relations rather than true piety.

Instead of spending all his energy defending himself, Moses decided to leave the matter with God. Tomorrow, the Lord said He would put an end to the dispute by distinguishing between the righteous and unrighteous. When unfairly attacked, sometimes the best thing a person can do is follow Moses' example and let God take care of it. The day of judgment will be the ultimate day of vindication for those who have lived faithfully.

THE PROBLEM OF UNGRATEFULNESS

Moses rebuked Korah for his ingratitude. Rather than appreciating the privilege of being a Levite, he grew increasingly jealous of those who served as priests. God separated the Levites from the general population and drew them near to Him by granting special permission to serve at the tabernacle. But discontentment robbed Korah of the joy and satisfaction he should have experienced. He viewed his role as insignificant when it was actually an exalted opportunity.

The problem of envy continues to cause unrest among the people of God. Paul taught that individual Christians are like parts of the human body (1 Corinthians 12:12-31). Each one is special and fulfills an important purpose. Men have a different role from women, and elders serve in a different capacity from deacons, but every function is vital to the health and well-being of the whole. To be jealous of one another is as senseless as an ear becoming upset because it is not an eye. Both are unique and indispensable.

A PUBLIC RELATIONS PLOY

Moses summoned Dathan and Abiram to meet with him personally, but they refused to appear. They defended their insubordination by circulating a rumor that Moses planned to gouge out their eyes (Numbers 16:14). The phrase might be taken symbolically in the sense of fooling or hoodwinking them, but it is not necessary to understand these words figuratively. They were probably hoping that the thought of one Israelite treating a brother so harshly would win public support for the rebellion.

Although Dathan and Abiram would not talk with Moses, they continued to talk about him. They accused him of bringing them out of a land of milk and honey rather than leading them to one. How quickly they had forgotten the bitterness of slavery and the policy of genocide they were subjected to in Egypt. From their perspective, the journey to Canaan was nothing more than a death march. It seemed like a suicide mission destined to fail. Saddest of all was their charge that Moses subjected them to the dangers of the desert because he was power hungry and wanted to lord his authority over them.

At that point, the meekest man in the world became upset. The job of national leader had been thrust upon Moses. He did not seek it, nor did he eagerly accept it. He had not robbed his people or wronged them in any way. To the contrary, he made many sacrifices to serve his countrymen, yet he was accused of taking personal advantage of his position and ruling in tyranny. Moses reminded Korah and his followers to prepare their censers and appear before the Lord the next day to settle this matter once and for all.

CENSER SHOWDOWN

The next morning, the glory of the Lord appeared at the tent of meeting. God told Moses and Aaron to separate themselves from the multitude because he was about to destroy them. Despite all he had suffered, Moses still loved the people of Israel and interceded on their behalf. His heart was filled with compassion, especially for those who had been misled by these cunning men. Moses warned everyone to move away from the rebels who stood defiantly at the entrance of their tents. Their smugness reminded Jude of the superior, self-righteous attitude he often saw in false teachers.

As the showdown began, Moses announced the criteria by which the people could know if he was sent by God to be their leader. If his opponents went unpunished and died a natural death, then Israel would know the Lord had not sent him. But if God did something totally new to punish them, it would be clear that they had treated the Lord with contempt by opposing him and Aaron.

Just as Moses finished his speech, the ground beneath the ringleaders split apart and swallowed them in darkness. The Israelites panicked and fled, fearing that the earth would engulf them too. In the meantime, fire came from the Lord and consumed the 250 supporters of Korah who were offering their incense.

A MESSAGE TO REBELS

God told Moses to have Eleazar collect the censers of the rebels who had sinned at the cost of their lives. The metal from the censers was hammered into sheets and used to overlay the altar. From then on, when anyone saw it, he was reminded of the folly of disobeying the authority of God.

The altar has long been gone, but the story of Korah will never be forgotten, thanks to the pen of Jude: "Woe to them! For they have … perished in the rebellion of Korah." The King James Version uses the word "gainsaying" in place of "rebellion." Gainsaying refers to opposing, contradicting or rejecting authority, especially to receive some personal advantage. False teachers who refuse to submit to rightful authority will perish in the end, just as Korah did.

Those who respect God should value leaders placed in positions of authority by Him. Children should honor and obey loving parents. Wives should submit to the headship of caring husbands. Saints should be model citizens who obey the laws of the land. Christians should respect and submit to the elders of the local church with whom they work and worship. Where these principles are followed, peace and harmony abound. Where they are ignored, broken homes, divided churches and disintegrating societies are found.

A MODEL OF RIGHTEOUSNESS

The techniques modeled by Moses for coping with unjustified criticism can be successfully employed by Christians today. When holy men and women find themselves under attack, they should pray to God for help in dealing with their enemies and their emotions. They should trust God to distinguish between the just and the unjust and to vindicate the righteous. Finally, they should separate themselves from spiritual insurrectionists to avoid being swallowed up in their sins.

Korah, like Cain and Balaam, was a highly religious man, yet he was far from righteous. What about you? Have you truly surrendered your life to God, or are you living in quiet rebellion? Are you satisfied with the opportunities and blessings He affords, or have worldly ambitions made you increasingly discontented and disagreeable?

CONTENTMENT VS. COMPLACENCY

God's patriots are people who are content to honor the Lord by doing their best in the role He has given them at the moment. They look forward to new opportunities but are also willing to let God open those doors when and where He sees fit. In the meantime, they are uniters rather than dividers. They cooperate with and support leaders rather than complain about them and scheme against them. They are energetic workers rather than envious whiners.

Those who serve Christ must be careful not to confuse contentment with complacency. God's people should continually be learning and growing in order to prepare themselves for greater service in the future. They ought to make high demands of themselves regardless of others' expectations. Christians, above all people, should be filled with drive and refuse merely to coast through life.

Saints who excel understand that ambition and submission are not mutually exclusive concepts. The key is to consecrate one's goals to God. Ambition is a virtue to the selfless, but a sin to the self-serving. It all depends on the motive. Why not genuinely submit your heart to God today and discover the happiness that comes from a life of full submission to His will? Do your best and let God take care of the rest.

DISCUSSION

1. Explain the term "gainsaying."

2. What did the rebels mean when they said Moses had gone too far?

3. Why do you suppose the rebel leaders refused to meet with Moses?

4. Why does the Bible refer to Moses as the meekest man on earth?

5. How do you think Moses felt after hearing the charges against him?

6. How did Moses deal with those who misrepresented him?

7. How can discontent rob a person of joy in life?

8. Why are those who are farthest from God frequently the boldest in claiming to know His will?

9. Why was the altar covered with the metal from the rebels' censers?

10. What should Christians learn from observing that Cain, Balaam and Korah were all highly religious people?

NINE
Analogies of Iniquity
Jude 12-13

If I am to know victory, I must never underestimate my enemy.

T he worst mistake a soldier can make is to underestimate his enemy. Jude was determined not to let this happen to his readers. Using all the imagination he could summon, he labored to describe the ruthlessness and corruption of false teachers who were threatening the church. He searched land, sky and sea to find the most appropriate images for illustrating their wickedness. In the end, he settled upon six powerful analogies to make his point.

SPOTS IN YOUR LOVE FEASTS

Jude began by comparing these corrupt men to "spots." They were human blemishes on the love feasts of the congregation. According to James, one of the essential elements of pure and undefiled religion is that Christians keep themselves "unspotted" from the world (James 1:27).

Paul used a wedding analogy to illustrate the importance of Christian purity. He wrote that Jesus gave Himself for the church, "that He might present her to Himself a glorious church, not having spot or wrinkle or any such thing, but that she should be holy and without blemish"

(Ephesians 5:27). Paul was comparing the church to an indigent bride who had undergone a special bath before being adorned with immaculate wedding garments in preparation for the ceremony. According to Paul's analogy, the bride's suitor, Jesus, provides both the bath and clothes for His beloved. At His crucifixion, Jesus gave Himself to cleanse and clothe destitute sinners who would unite their lives with Him in spiritual wedlock. It is a celestial rags-to-riches story unmatched in uninspired literature.

People who are added to the church are first *cleansed* from their past sins by contacting the blood of Jesus in the waters of baptism (Ephesians 5:26; Acts 2:38; 22:16; Romans 6:3; Hebrews 10:22). Immersion is also the act of initiation by which believers are clothed with Christ (Galatians 3:26-27). Baptism signifies an end to a person's love affair with sin. Paul was disturbed that some Christians did not understand the meaning of this universal conversion experience. Perplexed by increasing worldliness in the church, he asked, "How shall we who died to sin live any longer in it?" (Romans 6:2). Those who do not walk in newness of life are blemishes upon the church's reputation and fellowship (v. 4).

The "love feasts" Jude mentioned probably refer to the friendliness that was evident among saints as they enjoyed ordinary meals together. Luke highlighted the pleasure early Christians derived from this kind of fellowship: "So continuing daily with one accord in the temple, and breaking bread from house to house, they ate their food with gladness and simplicity of heart" (Acts 2:46). If these meals were in behalf of the poor or simply for congregational fellowship, they would be very similar to those that continue in churches today.

Some commentators believe the phrase "love feasts" is a reference to the weekly observance of the Lord's Supper (Acts 20:7). According to this view, the situation may have been similar to what occurred in Corinth where the memorial was corrupted and turned into a drunken feast (1 Corinthians 11:17-22). In either case, the point was the same. The sanctity of the occasion was diminished by the participation of false teachers.

Some translations use the word "rocks" instead of "spots" in Jude 12. Ungodly men are like hidden rocks along the shore that endanger the lives of seafarers. Both are difficult to recognize until it is too late. Sunken reefs have destroyed countless ships, and false teachers have shipwrecked the faith of many men (1 Timothy 1:19-20). Sailors and saints alike must be on constant lookout for concealed dangers that lie in wait.

SELF-SERVING SHEPHERDS

In a second analogy, Jude compared false teachers to self-centered shepherds who "feast with you without fear." They were consumed with satisfying their own egos and lusts while completely ignoring the spiritual needs of those entrusted to their care. "Without fear" suggests they were unconcerned about facing God in the judgment to account for their misdeeds.

Leaders are often called shepherds in Scripture. Ezekiel prophesied against the wicked shepherds of Israel and promised that God would hold them accountable for putting their own interests ahead of the people's welfare (Ezekiel 34). Jesus is called the Good Shepherd because He laid down His life for His sheep (John 10:11). His sacrificial love distanced Him from religious hirelings who cared only for themselves (v. 13).

Due to their influence, leaders can expect a higher level of accountability on the day of judgment (James 3:1; 1 Timothy 3:2). When a person proclaims himself a spiritual leader but does not live up to that trust, he has committed a serious offense. Whether the problem is apathy or opportunism, the outcome is the same.

CLOUDS WITHOUT WATER

Next, Jude painted a verbal portrait of false teachers as waterless clouds. It is doubtful that he envisioned white billowy clouds that lazily pass through the sky on a sunny day. It is more likely that he imagined dark clouds, always threatening rain but never delivering the refreshment so desperately needed.

Few things could be more disheartening in the dry arid regions of Judea than waterless clouds. Jude used this frustrating figure to portray the problem of spiritual drought. False teachers are like clouds that promise rain but never deliver. The book of Proverbs says, "Whosoever falsely boasts of giving is like clouds and wind without rain" (25:14).

These men were all talk and no show. Because living water was not within them, they had nothing to offer others.

The phrase "carried about by the winds" may symbolize the spiritual instability of ungodly men. The arguments of false teachers lack the integrity to withstand biblical doctrines. Jude could also be suggesting that these men were like clouds that create excitement as they come but leave disappointment as they go. When false teachers are finished, only parched souls are left in their wake.

TREES WITHOUT FRUIT

The fourth figure used of those undermining the faith was that of barren trees. Jude envisioned a person walking up to a fruit tree in late autumn expectantly looking forward to a ripe, juicy treat. Instead, the fruit was withered away, leaving the hungry individual bitterly disappointed. Such was the experience of those who sought spiritual food or blessing from these hypocrites.

Teachers who drink deeply from God's Word produce good fruit in abundance (Psalm 1:3). Knowing this, Jesus cautioned His disciples to appraise religious teachers by examining their fruits (Matthew 7:20). It is possible to know right from wrong, and those who embrace religious error will be held accountable because it was their responsibility to evaluate both the teaching and its source.

Jude used the phrase "twice dead" to depict the fruitless lives of false teachers. Perhaps he was expressing the fact that these men had sufficient time to prove themselves and had failed. Oftentimes, a tree that did not bear fruit one year was granted a reprieve until the next year. If no fruit was produced after two years, the tree was uprooted because it had no benefit. In this sense, it could be called twice dead. After two disappointing seasons, it was not only fruitless but also rootless. The remains would be burned, and a new tree would replace the old.

The phrase "twice dead" might also indicate the tragedy of Christians who had gone back into the world. Their predicament is powerfully portrayed in Hebrews 6:4-7. Nothing could be sadder than for a person to be saved from past sins only to be lost again at some future point. The second death awaits those whose transgressions have separated them from God. Whether "twice" suggests opportunity, apostasy or finality, it is clearly a modifier describing the more central idea of spiritual death.

John the Baptist told the Sadducees and Pharisees who came to his baptism that they must bring forth fruit worthy of repentance (Matthew 3:8). He added, "And even now the ax is laid to the root of the trees. Therefore every tree which does not bear good fruit is cut down and thrown into the fire" (v. 10).

In the closing days of Jesus' ministry, He noticed a fig tree with leaves but no fruit and used it to teach His disciples a valuable object lesson (Mark 11:12-14). Some Christians, like that tree, are not dead in appearance, yet neither are they fruitful. Saints who are all leaves (show) and no fruit (substance) will be judged in the same manner as the barren fig tree. Because it was unproductive, Jesus destroyed it, roots and all, indicating complete and final death.

RAGING WAVES

Jude turned to the "raging waves" for his next image of iniquity. The ungodly are wild and unstable like the tossing sea. Waves are noisy as they beat against the sand, yet for all their boisterousness, they produce nothing but a little foam that rides upon the crest. Similarly, false teachers are often loud and boastful, but for all their talk, they have little to show but the residue of their own shame.

Isaiah wrote, "But the wicked are like the troubled sea, When it cannot rest, Whose waters cast up mire and dirt" (Isaiah 57:20). Evil men are like the waves that bring in seaweed, driftwood and rubbish to pollute the beach after a storm. Instead of littering beaches, false teachers litter the minds and lives of those they influence. In some cases they are like giant waves that leave utter destruction in their path.

WANDERING STARS

Jude's final example of iniquity comes from the heavens. He likened false teachers to "wandering stars" reserved for the blackest darkness. Religious teachers are like stars because they impart the light of knowledge, but Jude had a special way of portraying those who distort the truth.

"Wandering" seems to refer to meteorites that blaze impressively across the horizon. Other stars are so fixed in orbit that they can be used for navigation. No one steers by meteorites for very long. Meteorites blaze furiously for a moment, but then their light is gone forever. These men were spiritual shooting stars. Their lights went out as they departed from God's will.

False teachers have wandered from the will of God. Their lives are spiritually off course. They can be impressive at times, but it is a mistake to look to them for direction. They are useless and untrustworthy. Unlike the star of Bethlehem, they cannot guide earthly sojourners to Christ or the safety of heaven.

Those who are faithful to God shine like stars in the midst of a sinful world (Philippians 2:15). They are people of enormous influence for good in the lives of others. In startling contrast, Jude described the lives and common destiny of false teachers in terms of darkness. The blackest darkness is reserved for those whose sins separate themselves from the one who is light (1 John 1:5). Once extinguished, falling stars do not regenerate their light. Likewise, the disobedient will discover that continual darkness is part of the misery of hell.

UNDERESTIMATING EVIL

It is a terrible blunder to underestimate one's adversary in battle. That is why New Testament writers have gone to great lengths to provide intelligence on the enemies of Christ. In a briefing session with the Ephesians, Paul supplied vital background information on the forces of Satan. He declared, "For we do not wrestle against flesh and blood, but against principalities, against powers, against the rulers of the darkness of this age, against spiritual hosts of wickedness in the heavenly places" (Ephesians 6:12).

In writing his battle plan for Christian warfare, Jude painted a vivid picture of the awfulness of sin and those who promote it. Its nature, effects and consequences were described in a graphic way that no one could misunderstand. False teachers are spiritually empty, fruitless, unstable, self-centered men. Their wild actions defile, disappoint, pollute, shame and destroy those whom they are able to influence. Death and darkness await those who have been uprooted from the faith once delivered unto the saints.

Faithful teachers of God's Word are the antithesis of Jude's macabre masterpiece. They are pure, refreshing, unselfish, fruitful, calm and stable. The joy and beauty of heaven await those who remain true to God's Word (Ephesians 4:17-19).

FRAMING FALSE TEACHING

When the queen of Sheba traveled to Jerusalem to witness the wisdom of Solomon, she exclaimed, "[I]ndeed the half was not told me" (1 Kings 10:7). So it is with the good news of Christ. The half has not been told of God's love, heaven's beauty or the gospel's power to save. Yet in the same way, preaching has done little more than scratch the surface when it comes to describing the awfulness of sin. Jude understood that feeling of inadequacy when he attempted to characterize false teachers who were troubling the church.

Overcoming evil requires facing the problem squarely. That is why it is a terrible mistake to downplay the danger of heresy. Jude understood the temptation to minimize the threat posed by such likeable people as the false teachers. Although it is admirable to bear with the misunderstandings of the weak, it is inexcusable to make light of the maneuverings of the willful.

Like Jude, spiritual patriots must honestly assess, accurately describe and graphically portray the wickedness of those who promote destructive beliefs. To oppose vigorously those who advocate error is neither unchristian nor unloving. It is regretful, yet absolutely necessary, to halt the harmful effects of false teaching. It is essential to protect the unity of the church and to preserve the purity of the faith and thus the only reasonable and responsible course to pursue.

Complainers who find fault with everything are not to be admired, but spiritual patriots who alert the church to real doctrinal danger are heroes of the faith and should be thanked for their courage and candidness. Do not ignore the problem of false teaching. It will not go away by itself. Tell it like it is so others can see it like it is. Jude did. Will you?

DISCUSSION

1. How difficult is it to describe the awfulness of sin?

2. How are false teachers like "spots"?

3. What were the "love feasts" Jude mentioned?

4. What word do some translations put in place of "spots"? Explain.

5. Why are religious leaders frequently compared to shepherds?

6. What did Jude mean when he said false teachers "feast with you without fear"?

7. How can false teachers be compared to waterless clouds?

8. How are false teachers like barren trees, twice dead, pulled up by the roots?

9. In what way are false teachers like "raging waves"?

10. How are false teachers like "wandering stars"?

TEN

The Lord Is Coming

Jude 14-16

If I am to know victory, I must prepare daily for Jesus' return.

When a high-ranking official arrives in a military camp, it is a time of anxiousness for enlisted men and officers alike. Inspections and parades are the order of the day. Some soldiers are fearful, and others are hopeful, depending on their state of preparedness.

INSPECTION TIME

Jude reminded his readers of an impending inspection by their commander-in-chief – Jesus. Jude's information came from the Old Testament prophet Enoch, who foretold that the Lord was coming to review His troops and reward them accordingly. At that time, faithful men and women will be commended, but those who have engaged in insubordination and disorderly conduct will be summarily punished.

Enoch is one of the most fascinating lesser-known characters in the Bible. He is first mentioned by Moses in Genesis 5:21-24:

> Enoch lived sixty-five years, and begot Methuselah. After he begot Methuselah, Enoch walked with God three hun-

dred years, and had sons and daughters. So all the days of Enoch were three hundred and sixty-five years. And Enoch walked with God; and he was not, for God took him.

The writer of Hebrews supplemented the record of Enoch's life with these additional words: "By faith Enoch was taken away so that he did not see death, 'and was not found, because God had taken him'; for before he was taken he had this testimony, that he pleased God" (Hebrews 11:5).

In confronting the false teachers of his day, Jude cited a prophecy attributed to this holy man of God who withstood evil in his own time. When Jude contemplated the corruption he saw spreading through the church, he found encouragement by reflecting on Enoch's reassuring words. Enoch, who knew God more intimately than any man of his day, promised that the Lord would not allow evil to triumph. He had no doubt that God would punish the wicked and reward the faithful. Under the direction of the Holy Spirit, Jude applied these words to evil men in the first century.

"BEHOLD, THE LORD COMES"

The opening line of Enoch's prophecy declared "Behold, the Lord comes" (Jude 14). The Lord's coming return is an event all people desperately need to "behold" (take serious note of). Unless a person comes to grips with the certainty of this event, there is no hope in eternity.

Enoch said the Lord's return is more than a possibility. It is guaranteed! The New Testament is equally adamant on this point. Jesus promised that if He went to prepare a place in heaven for His followers, they could count on Him to come back and get them (John 14:1-4). It is not a question of if but when (Matthew 24:36; 1 Thessalonians 5:1-2).

The apostles constantly reminded Christians to live in view of the Lord's return. Paul used the familiar Aramaic term *maranatha* (our Lord, come!) to remind his readers that Jesus' second coming was approaching (1 Corinthians 16:22). Those who anticipate Christ's triumphant return find the strength they need to endure life's trials and temptations. Paul boasted, "[F]or I know whom I have believed and am persuaded that He is able to keep what I have committed to Him until that Day" (2 Timothy 1:12).

"WITH TEN THOUSANDS OF HIS SAINTS"

When Jesus does return, He will not be alone. Enoch disclosed that He will be accompanied by "ten thousands of His saints." The term "saints" refers to the holy ones who will escort Jesus to earth. A similar phrase was used by Moses when he blessed the Israelites saying, "The Lord came from Sinai, And dawned on them from Seir; He shone forth from Mount Paran, And He came with ten thousands of saints" (Deuteronomy 33:2). The prophet Zechariah also spoke of these attendants of the Lord. He wrote, "Then you shall flee through my mountain valley; For the mountain valley shall reach to Azal. Yes, you shall flee, As you fled from the earthquake in the days of Uzziah king of Judah. Thus the Lord my God will come, And all the saints with you" (Zechariah 14:5).

The New Testament writers confirm that Jesus will not be alone when He returns. The Lord spoke plainly of angels accompanying Him when He comes to separate the righteous from the wicked in preparation for judgment (Matthew 25:31). Paul announced that the archangel will be among Jesus' holy assistants and that his voice will be heard throughout the earth (1 Thessalonians 4:16). In another letter, he described the day when mighty angels will be revealed from heaven as Jesus comes to take vengeance upon those who have persecuted and troubled His followers (2 Thessalonians 1:7-9).

"TO EXECUTE JUDGMENT"

One of the primary reasons for Jesus' return will be to "execute judgment." The apostle John recorded several significant details of that event in his own book of prophecy. He wrote, "And I saw the dead, small and great, standing before God, and books were opened. And another book was opened, which is the Book of Life. And the dead were judged according to their works, by the things which were written in the books" (Revelation 20:12).

All people will be judged impartially by God without regard to their social standing. The dead will be raised bodily and take their place beside the living to account for their works. Two books will play a critical role in man's judgment. One is identified as the Book of Life in which the names of heaven's citizens have been recorded. The other book remains a mystery.

Could the second book contain the names of citizens of hell? Is it a journal preserving an accurate record of human deeds upon the earth? Could it be a copy of the Scriptures, the standard by which all people will be judged?

Although it is impossible to be dogmatic in identifying the second book, the third alternative has much to recommend it. In his gospel narrative, John recalled Jesus' pronouncement that His words would judge mankind on the last day (John 12:48). As the Lord assesses people's lives, their eternal destiny will be directly related to their willingness to submit to the teaching of the Bible.

One thing is certain. When the Lord returns to execute judgment, there will be no favoritism and no mistakes. That is why Paul fondly called God the righteous Judge (2 Timothy 4:8). He will bring the most secret sins to light on that day. Sins not publicly known or privately repented of at the time of an individual's death will follow him into judgment where they will be exposed. All wrongs will be righted by the Son of Man who has been given authority to execute judgment (John 5:27).

God is neither careless nor corrupt. There will be no injustice in His judgment as is sometimes the case on earth. On that day, there will be no plea bargaining, no "taking the fifth," no appeals to a higher court. Justice will be served.

"TO CONVICT ALL WHO ARE UNGODLY"

Enoch said that when judgment does occur the ungodly will finally be convinced of their folly (Jude 15). The most prominent word in Jude's epistle is "ungodly," which refers to those who have no respect for the Lord or sacred things. They live as if there is no God, no judgment and no hell. The time is coming when they will learn otherwise.

There is nothing like a moment in hell to "convict" a person that the Bible is true. When he awoke in torment, it took only an instant for the rich man to learn the error of his materialistic, self-indulgent lifestyle. When he begged for Lazarus to be sent to warn his brothers, Abraham told him, "They have Moses and the prophets; let them hear them" (Luke 16:29). One purpose of God's Word is to convince men of their need to prepare for judgment to avoid the painful and unnecessary experience of eternal punishment. Tragically, many people insist on learning this lesson the hard way.

Jesus spoke of those who will be shocked to awaken in agony after the completion of their earthly sojourn. He declared, "Many will say to Me in that day, 'Lord, Lord, have we not prophesied in Your name, cast out demons in Your name, and done many wonders in Your name?' And then I will declare to them, 'I never knew you; depart from Me, you who practice lawlessness!' " (Matthew 7:22-23). Being religious is clearly not the same thing as being righteous.

Consider, for example, Jesus' parable of the publican and the Pharisee. Envision the Pharisee confidently sweeping up the stairs of the temple, robe flowing, as he found a suitable place to be observed by his fellow worshipers. He prayed, "God, I thank You that I am not like other men – extortioners, unjust, adulterers, or even as this tax collector. I fast twice a week; I give tithes of all that I possess" (Luke 18:11-12).

Not once did he ask for divine assistance. No sin was confessed. No plea was made for mercy. Nothing could be more ungodly than the arrogance of one who comes into God's presence exalting himself. The Pharisee, and those like him, will be convinced at the judgment of the true meaning of godliness and their own need for God's grace.

WHAT WILL GOD JUDGE?

• **Works.** Enoch stressed that two things will be called into judgment: a man's words and his works. By examining these, God will assess each man's status and determine his destiny. The prudent will inspect their own lives before judgment to please God and prepare for that day (2 Timothy 2:4; 3:16; 1 Thessalonians 4:1-2).

The Bible is clear that a man's deeds will play a major role in determining his eternal destiny. Paul wrote, "For we must all appear before the judgment seat of Christ, that each one may receive the things done in the body, according to what he has done, whether good or bad" (2 Corinthians 5:10). James declared, "You see then that a man is justified by works, and not by faith only" (James 2:24). The apostle John recorded, "The sea gave up the dead who were in it, and Death and Hades delivered up the dead who were in them. And they were judged, each one according to his works" (Revelation 20:13).

No one can earn entrance into heaven by good deeds, but humble obedience to Christ's teaching is necessary for salvation. Christians must account for their conduct just like everyone else. God will forgive sin but not wink at it. In fact, the Lord expects more from His children because of their advantages. God does not require sinless perfection for salvation, but He does demand that people's lives demonstrate the genuineness of their faith and love.

Man is saved by faith, but the crucial evidence of faith is one's works. What is obedience but faith in action? Disobedience, on the other hand, contradicts and repudiates faith. Those who heed God's Word honor Him and discover the joy of abundant life in so doing.

• **Words.** The other thing to be called into judgment is a person's words. Jude said that false teachers will have to account for the harsh things they have spoken against God. They may have attacked God personally, but all forms of sinful speech are against Him indirectly.

Christ established a correlation between judgment and human speech. When the Pharisees blasphemed the Holy Spirit by attributing Jesus' miracles to an evil spirit, the Lord pointed out the seriousness of their charge. Imagine how human communication would differ if people really took these words to heart?

> Brood of vipers! How can you, being evil, speak good things? For out of the abundance of the heart the mouth speaks. A good man out of the good treasure of his heart brings forth good things, and an evil man out of the evil treasure brings forth evil things. But I say to you that for every idle word men may speak, they will give account of it in the day of judgment. For by your words you will be justified, and by your words you will be condemned. (Matthew 12:34-37)

The apostles instructed Christians to pay careful attention to their speech. A saint's words should be pure and beneficial, not corrupt and detrimental (Ephesians 4:29). Paul encouraged believers to season their speech with salt (Colossians 4:6). Even truthful talk should be flavored with kindness. A message is more palatable when words and tone are carefully selected (Matthew 7:12).

Nothing is more revealing of man's heart and religion than his day-to-day conversation. James declared, "If anyone among you thinks he is religious, and does not bridle his tongue but deceives his own heart, this one's religion is useless. Pure and undefiled religion before God and the Father is this: to visit orphans and widows in their trouble, and to keep oneself unspotted from the world" (James 1:26-27). Actions, not intentions, will form the basis of God's judgment. Words and works are the test of true religion, and every person will account for his on the last day.

THINGS TO AVOID

Jude provided several examples of ungodly words and works that ought to be avoided by his readers. These traits were typical of the false teachers in their midst. "Grumblers" (Jude 16) were modern counterparts of the rebellious Israelites whose ill-tempered mumbling could be heard throughout the desert wanderings. "Complainers" referred to malcontents who were chronically dissatisfied with everything.

No doubt people are more susceptible to error when they are discouraged. That is why false teachers try to stir up discontent within churches they seek to influence. Busy, happy people are resistant to heresy. Congregations where Christians are hypercritical are more susceptible to sin and schism.

Ungodly people are also those who "walk according to their own lusts" (Jude 16). The flesh rather than the Spirit serves as their compass in life (James 1:12-17). This kind of lifestyle was renounced by Paul in his letter to Titus: "For the grace of God that brings salvation has appeared to all men, teaching us that, denying ungodliness and worldly lusts, we should live soberly, righteously, and godly in the present age" (Titus 2:11-12).

Others are distinguished for speaking "great swelling words" (Jude 16). This means that they sought to justify their worldliness with empty orations. With an impressive vocabulary and powerful delivery, they defended themselves and belittled their opponents. They were imposing, moving speakers who used their refined skills to dispute simple New Testament teaching.

Jude ended by portraying false teachers as fawning parasites, "flat-

tering people to gain advantage." They were opportunists who court-
ed rich, influential people for their own benefit. Their attitude was far
different from Paul who believed that godliness with contentment is
great gain (1 Timothy 6:6). Faithful Christians must not lose the will
to discern what is right rather than what is profitable.

FINAL INSPECTION

Anticipating the supreme commander's return, spiritual patriots must
remain at a high state of readiness at all times. To prepare for that day,
soldiers of Christ undergo continual training in godliness (1 Timothy
4:8). Those in search of this precious training can find all they need to
know in the pages of the Bible (2 Peter 1:3). Peter used the approaching end of the world as a powerful motivation to develop this trait:
"Therefore, since all these things will be dissolved, what manner of
persons ought you to be in holy conduct and godliness, looking for and
hastening the coming of the day of God, because of which the heavens
will be dissolved, being on fire, and the elements will melt with fervent heat?" (3:11-12). The information and incentive needed to live a
godly life have been provided by God, but each believer must avail
himself of it. Are you prepared for final inspection?

DISCUSSION

1. Who was Enoch?

2. Describe the second coming of Jesus.

3. What reason does Enoch mention for the Lord's coming?

4. What information does the Bible provide about the judgment?

5. How will God "convict" false teachers of their ungodliness?

6. Because Christians are saved by grace, how can their works have
   a bearing on their judgment and eternal destiny?

7. What role will a person's words play in judgment?

8. Why are false teachers said to speak "great swelling words"?

9. How are false teachers guilty of "flattering people to gain advantage"?

10. How does God provide mankind with the information and incentive needed to live godly lives?

ELEVEN

Defeating Discouragement

Jude 17-19

If I am to know victory, I must not be easily disheartened.

D iscouragement is one of the most effective weapons in Satan's arsenal. If he can convince struggling saints that it is futile to battle immorality and error, they will often grow weary and give up. Jude anticipated that possibility and assured his readers there was no reason to despair.

"But you, beloved, remember the words which were spoken before by the apostles of our Lord Jesus Christ" (Jude 17). Earlier, Jude told his readers to remember Israel's history that showed how God dealt with wickedness in the past. Later, he reminded them of Enoch's prophecy disclosing what God will do with ungodly men in the future. Finally, Jude called to mind a sobering prediction made by the apostles within their own lifetime.

REMEMBER THE APOSTLES' WORDS

Jude asked his readers to search their memories and recall that the apostles forewarned them that false teachers would flourish until Jesus' return. Christians should not be taken by surprise when false teaching arises within the church. Paul told the Ephesian elders that grievous wolves would arise among them to attack and devour the flock under their care (Acts 20:20-30). John, the apostle of love, spoke of numerous antichrists who operated from within the ranks of the redeemed. Peter announced, "[T]here will be false teachers among you, who will secretly bring in destructive heresies, even denying the Lord who bought them, and bring on themselves swift destruction" (2 Peter 2:1). Christians were never instructed to put blind trust in religious leaders.

It is significant that Jude spoke of the apostles' (plural) words rather than an apostle's (singular) words. Warnings against spiritual insurrection in the church are by no means isolated. The apostles were united in an effort to prepare believers to face this potentially demoralizing problem. The fact that Jude reminded his readers of these warnings meant that they had either heard or read them for themselves at some earlier time. Those words must not be forgotten! What had been warned against was now coming to pass.

Nothing is more discouraging than opposition from within, especially when leaders such as elders, teachers, youth ministers and preachers are involved. Disillusionment and despair can overwhelm an individual or an entire church. Jude believed that if Christians would keep the apostles' words in mind, it would help them defeat discouragement.

Jude wanted to protect his readers against unrealistic expectations about the church and religious leaders. Saints should be saddened but not shocked when those who claim to be Christians advocate some form of immorality or doctrinal error. Regretfully, this is to be expected.

Christians who have romantic notions about a sinlessly perfect church or its leadership are easy prey for Satan. The divine design of the church is flawless, but human beings often fall short of God's plan. When confronted by ungodliness within a local church, idealistic individuals may lose their faith or go into denial. Faith must be centered in Christ rather than in men or institutions.

THEY TOLD YOU THERE WOULD BE MOCKERS

Jude went on to refer to a particular kind of ungodliness the apostles had spoken about. These holy men foretold the emergence of mockers in the last time. One of the indispensable duties of religious leaders is to forewarn the people about God. Although all Christians are commanded to exhort one another daily, God will demand an accounting of those in positions of leadership that transcends the spontaneous counsel of brothers in Christ. Some elders and preachers have mistakenly assumed that their responsibility is to avoid controversy and keep peace at any cost.

Paul tearfully warned the Ephesians day and night for three years (Acts 20:31). He informed the Corinthians, "I do not write these things to shame you, but as my beloved children I warn you" (1 Corinthians 4:14). Paul told the Colossians that he preached Christ, warning every man (Colossians 1:28). Jude's epistle, replete with warnings, is a classic example of this spiritual obligation.

The apostles specifically mentioned that scoffers will appear in the "last time." This phrase was a common way of referring to the Christian age. The writer of Hebrews called his lifetime "these last days" (Hebrews 1:1-2). That period was characterized by Christ's teaching, as contrasted with the law of Moses.

On Pentecost, Peter told the multitude that Joel's prophecy concerning the last days was being fulfilled before their very eyes (Acts 2:16-17). Similarly, in referring to the apostles' words, Jude was saying that what they had spoken of was now taking place. Christianity, the golden age of humanity, would not be a utopia on earth. Despite the privileges and blessings it afforded mankind, some would continue to live in rebellion and contradict sound doctrine – even some professed believers!

The likelihood of false teachers emerging in the last days was more than a probability. Jude said the apostles were absolutely clear on this point. There will be scoffers! Of this, there can be no doubt.

DEALING WITH DERISION

"Mockers" (Jude 18) are those who ridicule or make fun of sacred things. They are often characterized by an arrogant, condescending attitude. What should Christians do when confronted by people who laugh at their convictions?

First, they should keep their composure and not become alarmed. Rage and hysteria are not effective in the fight against false teaching.

Poise, on the other hand, is a very powerful weapon in the arsenal of truth. Jude was saying in effect, "Do not panic! Do not be deterred! Do not let them shake your faith!" Second, they should remember what God has done and promised to keep doing about the problem of ungodliness. "Surely he scorns the scornful" (Proverbs 3:34). In due time, He will deal with those who mock truth. Christians should not allow a person under divine indictment to demoralize their faith.

SCOFFING AT THE SECOND COMING

Although Jude did not specify what these scoffers were mocking, Peter did designate a particular item of faith ridiculed by the false teachers he encountered. In 2 Peter 3:1-4 he stated:

> Beloved, I now write to you this second epistle (in both of which I stir up your pure minds by way of reminder), that you may be mindful of the words which were spoken before by the holy prophets, and of the commandment of us, the apostles of the Lord and Savior, knowing this first: that scoffers will come in the last days, walking according to their own lusts, and saying, "Where is the promise of His coming? For since the fathers fell asleep, all things continue as they were from the beginning of creation."

Supposed Christians were scoffing at those who believed in Jesus' second coming and the final judgment of mankind. Peter accused these men of willfully ignoring the certainty of these events to excuse their ungodly lifestyles (2 Peter 3:1-7). There was clearly a motive behind their madness.

Peter explained that God's delay should be equated with patience rather than slackness. God is not late – He is longsuffering! The only reason God waits to execute judgment is because He loves us so dearly. He wants to give people every opportunity to repent and avoid eternal punishment. Therefore, holiness and godliness are in order.

Earlier in his letter, Jude stated that false teachers were turning the grace of God into lewdness (v. 4). The reason they attacked sacred beliefs was to defend and excuse some form of promiscuous behavior. When Jude said they "walk according to their own ungodly lusts" (v. 18) he was indicating that their doctrine was nothing more than a reflection of their desires.

Mockery is one of the favorite tools of false teachers. Because what they wish to promote cannot be sustained on the basis of reasoned evidence, they must resort to a lower means of persuasion. It is clearly an admission that their beliefs lack a proper biblical basis.

SEPARATE AND SENSUAL

Still, these ungodly men were boldly claiming spiritual superiority over faithful teachers. Jude wrote, "These are sensual persons, who cause divisions, not having the Spirit" (v. 19). Their strategy was to divide and conquer the community of believers by accentuating their differences. Charging their adversaries with ignorance and intolerance, they confused people's minds and gained a following. From a human standpoint, it was an ingenious plan, but as James said, "This wisdom does not descend from above" (James 3:15).

Jude emphasized that these ungodly false teachers were motivated by sensuality rather than sincere beliefs. Gratification was valued above sanctification. They were preoccupied with the body rather than the soul and the present more than the future. Although they claimed to be spiritual giants, they operated more like animals. Their audacity was a testimony to their shamelessness.

Today as then, it is not uncommon for false teachers to boast of special insight into God's loving character to make light of departures from His Word. They specialize in emotional manipulation rather than biblical interpretation. Theatrics and debate tactics are substituted for honest exegesis of pertinent texts. Sadly, growing numbers of Christians are susceptible to these devices due to rising biblical illiteracy. Celebrity is valued more than veracity, feelings are prized above faith, and experience is preferred to exegesis.

There was no excuse for being deceived by these masqueraders. The apostles used the plainest possible language to prevent honest people from being misled. Paul wrote, "For if you live according to the flesh you will die; but if by the Spirit you put to death the deeds of the body, you will live" (Romans 8:13).

Paul provided the churches of Galatia with a representative list of sins to be avoided by Christians:

> Now the works of the flesh are evident, which are: adultery, fornication, uncleanness, lewdness, idolatry, sorcery, hatred, contentions, jealousies, outbursts of wrath, selfish ambitions, dissensions, heresies, envy, murders, drunkenness, revelries, and the like; of which I tell you beforehand, just as I also told you in time past, that those who practice such things will not inherit the kingdom of God. (Galatians 5:19-21)

The apostle was describing the activities of men and women who yield to the impulses of their lower nature. These works of the flesh are commonly classified into four groups: sins related to sexuality, superstition, anger and alcohol.

Although false teachers claimed to be directed by the Spirit, Jude pointed to their conduct as evidence to the contrary. In writing to the Galatians, Paul explained that the cultivation of a virtuous life is evidence of the Spirit's influence: "But the fruit of the Spirit is love, joy, peace, longsuffering, kindness, goodness, faithfulness, gentleness, self-control. Against such there is no law" (Galatians 5:22-23).

Near the end of Jude's letter, he instructed his readers to pray in the Spirit. This was his way of reminding them that they were the ones truly in fellowship with God, rather than the sensual cynics who scoffed at their faith. They needed to continue to trust in God, live holy lives, and refuse to be disheartened by the insults of religious charlatans.

YOU CAN DEFEAT DISCOURAGEMENT!

Satan has mastered the art of psychological warfare, but Christians can defeat discouragement by remembering the apostles' words. There will always be mockers who attempt to dishearten the faithful by sneering at sound doctrine. Do not let the devil's propaganda diminish your will to stand firm in the face of false teaching. May God's promise of victory fill your heart with the courage and confidence you need to continue the good fight to its end.

DISCUSSION

1. How does Satan use discouragement to defeat struggling saints?

2. Why should Christians not be surprised when false teaching arises within the church or Christian schools?

3. What significance is there in the fact that Jude spoke of remembering the apostles' (plural) words rather than a single apostle's words?

4. How can unrealistic expectations of church leaders be dangerous?

5. What did Jude mean by the "last days"?

6. How do mockers undermine Christian faith?

7. Why do false teachers resort to mockery?

8. How and why do mockers cause division?

9. Why was Jude convinced that these false teachers did not have the Spirit?

10. How should Christians react to those who scoff at sound doctrine?

TWELVE

Build Yourselves Up

Jude 20-23

If I am to know victory, I must accept personal
responsibility for my spiritual growth.

Nearly three quarters of Jude's epistle was dedicated to providing vivid descriptions of the danger his readers were facing. If he accomplished nothing else, he would be sure that they did not underestimate the seriousness of their predicament or their adversaries. As he neared the end of the letter, he turned his attention to practical instruction for those whose faith was under assault. What should Christians do when finding themselves confronted by worldliness in the church?

BUILD YOURSELF UP

Jude's first advice was to build yourself up on your most holy faith (v. 20). When problems are properly addressed, they are not insurmountable obstacles but rather opportunities in disguise. In the midst of trials and turmoil, there is tremendous potential for personal growth. It all depends on one's attitude (James 1:2-5).

The Bible frequently speaks of spiritual growth in terms of building. The Hebrews writer compared immature Christians to an unfinished structure consisting of a foundation with no superstructure (Hebrews 6:1). He exhorted them to complete what they had begun by building their spiritual lives tall and strong for God's glory. Both individually and collectively, the church should always be growing in this way.

Jude placed the responsibility for such growth squarely on the shoulders of his readers. That did not mean he expected them to do it alone but that even with God's help it would require a serious effort on their part. God has provided every encouragement and resource necessary for mature development, but saints must take advantage of the means He makes available. The cooperative nature of this enterprise is evident from Paul's command to "work out your own salvation with fear and trembling; for it is God who works in you both to will and to do for His good pleasure" (Philippians 2:12-13). Christians must build themselves up.

The foundation of all such building is "faith" in Christ. There is some question as to what kind of faith is called for here. Does Jude speak of objective or subjective faith? Does he refer to personal belief or what is believed? Both are necessary for any real growth to occur, and both are implied by this passage. How can people be built up if they have the right information but do not believe it? How can they advance spiritually by believing, however deeply, in the wrong thing? True progress demands deep personal trust in Christ and His teaching.

Paul indicated in Romans 10:17 that the source of faith is the Word of God. That means Christians must build themselves up by studying the Bible. In preparing the Ephesian elders to withstand false teaching, Paul said, "I commend you to God and to the word of His grace, which is able to build you up" (Acts 20:32).

Jude called this faith "most holy" (v. 20). Holiness indicates that something is sacred or special. The Sabbath was holy because it was unlike any other day of the week. The temple was called holy because it was different from all other buildings. The Bible is holy because no other book in the entire world is like it.

Faith, whether objective or subjective, is most holy in a number of ways. It is special because of its source: divine revelation. It is unique because of its power to save souls and transform lives. Those who pos-

sess faith are different from those without it. They are distinct in the
One they worship and in the way they worship. They are different
because of their values and standards. They are in but not of the world
as indicated by the name "saint" meaning "separated one."

PRAY IN THE SPIRIT

Jude's second admonition was for Christians to pray (v. 20). The
need for constancy in prayer can hardly be overemphasized. Both Jesus
and the apostles stressed the value of this spiritual discipline (Luke
18:1-8; 1 Thessalonians 5:17).

Jude's friends had many things to pray about because of the ordeals
they were facing. They needed to pray for the church and its elders in
the midst of this crisis. They needed to pray for their enemies, asking
God to thwart their purpose and soften their hearts. They needed to ask
for personal strength to remain faithful and boldly defend sound doctrine. They needed divine assistance in edifying the saved and recov-
ering the lost. Spiritual patriots must have access to God's power if
they are to be victorious.

Jude called on his readers to pray "in the Holy Spirit" (v. 20). It is
possible that he was referring to the exercise of miraculous power available in the first century (1 Corinthians 14:14). Such a conclusion is not
certain, however, because whatever Christians do should be done in the
Spirit. Paul called for believers to walk in or be led by the Spirit
(Galatians 5:16, 18). Whenever an act of love or kindness manifests itself in the lives of God's people, it is equally an act of the Spirit
(vv. 22-25). Loving and praying, although non-miraculous, are divinely
induced behaviors of God-filled people. Every biblical mandate is root-
ed in inspiration; therefore, any act of obedience may be attributed to
the Holy Spirit who prompted it.

A third possibility is that Jude was talking about a special kind of
communication that occurs between the Spirit and God when saints
engage in earnest prayer (Romans 8:26). Because it is difficult to as-
certain Jude's precise meaning, it is probably more beneficial to engage in praying rather than lingering over fine details of the Spirit's
involvement in communication that is indiscernible to the human
senses. Suffice it to say that "the effective, fervent prayer of a right-

eous man avails much" (James 5:16). With the encouragement of the Holy Spirit, how could it not be so?

KEEP YOURSELVES IN GOD'S LOVE

Jude's third instruction was for Christians to "keep" themselves in the love of God (v. 21). John wrote, "For this is the love of God, that we keep His commandments. And His commandments are not burdensome" (1 John 5:3). God's love may also refer to the Lord's love for man. Obedience is the proper response in either case. Jesus declared, "If you keep My commandments, you will abide in My love, just as I have kept My Father's commandments and abide in His love" (John 15:10). Intimacy with God requires submission, not just sentiment.

Ancient Israel entered into a covenant relationship with God that was founded on and maintained by love. God's love was demonstrated in the exodus and in the provision of laws designed to promote a happy, holy life for the nation. The people were to return God's love by faithfully observing the stipulations of the covenant. When the Israelites kept God's commands they were blessed, but when they disobeyed His laws they were punished. Similarly, Christians must maintain their relationship with God through honoring His covenant commands revealed in the New Testament.

Men like Noah, Joseph, Samuel and Daniel obeyed God in times of extreme difficulty. Their stories are preserved in Scripture to assure men and women that they can do the same. Faithfulness is possible in the worst of circumstances thanks to the help God provides.

LOOK FOR MERCY

Jude's fourth point was for his friends to remember that people at their very best still need *mercy* (v. 21). Christians should work hard and pray hard, but they will never reach sinless perfection in this lifetime. When personal failures do occur, penitence is in order, but despair is not.

As Christians watch and wait for Jesus' return, it is good to know He is not only a sovereign Lord but also a merciful Savior. Eternal life would be impossible otherwise (Titus 3:5). Maintaining a right standing with God does not require infallibility, but it is conditioned upon godliness (2:11-14).

First-century Christians constantly lived with the Lord's return in view. It was a powerful incentive to purify their lives and immerse themselves in doing good (1 John 3:1-3). The absence of this air of expectancy can explain the rise of worldliness within the church today.

"ON SOME HAVE COMPASSION"

Jude's fifth and final exhortation was for his readers to be merciful to others (v. 22). In the Sermon on the Mount, Jesus linked a person's happiness to his compassion for his fellowman: "Blessed are the merciful, For they shall obtain mercy" (Matthew 5:7). James indicated that a lack of consideration for others would also have a bearing on one's eternal destiny: "For judgment is without mercy to the one who has shown no mercy" (James 2:13). This was precisely the case of the rich man who woke to find himself in torment due to his neglect of the beggar Lazarus (Luke 16:24). These verses help to explain why Christ classified mercy as one of the weightier matters of the law (Matthew 23:23).

If it is good to extend mercy to others in times of physical need (Luke 10:30-37), how much more should it be shown in times of spiritual need? Jude used this trait to describe the proper response his readers should have toward those influenced by false teachers. Mercy does not negate accountability. Rather, it holds people accountable in the most loving and supportive way. Mercy does not demand its pound of flesh. It seeks beneficial change in those whose thinking and behavior are errant.

Jude called on mature Christians to be merciful to those who doubt (Jude 22). It is crucial to understand the difference between doubt and unbelief. Doubt involves momentary confusion while unbelief is more of a settled conviction. Even great men like Elijah (1 Kings 19) and John the Baptist (Matthew 11:1-15) experienced brief bouts with doubt, but when they faced their fears and worked through them, their doubts became the means to a stronger faith. Uncertainty is usually the beginning of thought. Unbelief is typically the end of thought.

Those who doubt are not to be chided or chastised. People who are confused on some point of doctrine need the patience and kindness of those who are stronger in the faith. They are not to be berated or belittled because of their lack of understanding. Teaching and time will resolve most honest doubts. A spirit of gentleness in dealing with such matters is far more effective than intimidation.

On the other hand, there are times when subtlety simply will not do. If someone is asleep in a burning house, there is no time to rouse him gently from his slumber. Quick action must be taken in times of such urgency. This is clearly the case when a person has progressed beyond doubt to the very edge of the abyss of unbelief. Jude envisions the flames of hell flickering around the feet of one who is only a step away from falling into a chasm of iniquity from which he will never return. He must be snatched from the fire if he is to be saved. There is no time to wait a few months and see what happens. Swift action and straight talk are the only hope.

OTHERS SAVE WITH FEAR

Finally, Jude discussed the need for mercy in relating to the false teachers themselves. Christians are commanded by Christ to love their enemies, even those attacking the faith. It is possible to care deeply about an individual without approving of his or her actions.

Jude warned his friends to mix their merciful efforts to recover false teachers with fear for their own spiritual safety. How many times has someone attempted to save another person from physical danger only to be overcome himself! Love's reckless abandonment of concern for self is a magnificent display of what is best in man. However, greater caution is in order when the soul is placed in harm's way. An added measure of discretion is advisable lest Christians become partakers of the very sins from which they attempt to rescue others.

Jude illustrated his point by recalling how the Israelites were to deal with the dreaded disease of leprosy (Leviticus 13:47-52). One should be as cautious in attempts to recover certain classes of sinners as would be the case in helping someone with a highly contagious disease. In dealing with leprosy, even the clothes were to be burned. The point is that every precaution should be taken when dealing with the plague of sin. Different people require different approaches (patient, direct, cautious), but the common goal is to save the lost.

BACK TO BASICS

Jude offers a practical and positive approach to battling worldliness. As spiritual patriots await the return of Jesus, they should study often, pray without ceasing, obey God's commands, and be merciful to those in physical or spiritual need. These duties provide a fuller explanation of what Jude had in mind when he commanded Christians to contend for the faith. It is a call to return to the basics, not an excuse for rancor.

DISCUSSION

1. Why did Jude spend the majority of his letter imparting vivid descriptions of the false teachers and the certainty of their punishment?

2. How do trials offer tremendous potential for personal growth?

3. Where does Jude place the responsibility for spiritual growth? Why?

4. How can a Christian build himself up in the faith? Why does Jude call faith "most holy"?

5. What does it mean to pray "in the Holy Spirit" (Jude 20)? What kinds of things might Jude's readers pray about?

6. How can a Christian keep himself in the love of God?

7. How important is it for faithful, hardworking Christians to remember their own need for divine mercy?

8. How do circumstances affect evangelistic strategies?

9. How can trying to recover a person in sin be like dealing with leprosy?

10. How does Jude 20-23 summarize what it means to contend for the faith?

THIRTEEN

God Is Able

Jude 24-25

---

*If I am to know victory, I must trust God
to sustain me through trying times.*

The conclusion of a letter is often the climax. That was clearly the case with the epistle of Jude. Jude's letter began with a prayer for mercy, peace and love to be multiplied among the faithful remnant of believers. They were going to need that unity to fulfill his charge to contend for the faith once delivered unto the saints.

Next, Jude exhorted his readers not to be discouraged or swayed by the false teachers who had infiltrated their congregation. Regardless of how things looked at the moment, the ungodly would not prevail in the end. It was only a matter of time until they would be punished for the harm they were doing the church. Jude provided his readers with practical counsel on how to endure triumphantly during those difficult days.

Last, but not least, Jude pointed them to the power of God to sustain them in the midst of change and crisis in the church. He concluded his writing with a comforting prayer in behalf of battle-weary saints. Their struggle was too important for compromise or surrender. Although worn down, they must continue the good fight to the very end. Where could they find the help and strength so desperately needed at this critical time? Christians can count on God when the going gets tough.

TO HIM WHO IS ABLE

Jude began his prayer with the memorable phrase, "Now to Him who is able" (v. 24). Those words immediately bring to mind the glorious history of Israel and the impressive way God has taken care of His covenant people through the ages. Time and again, the Lord rescued them from their enemies and blessed them in their obedience. Two outstanding episodes from the book of Daniel illustrate God's ability to help His people in trying times.

• **God Saves From the Fiery Furnace.** The first incident occurred on the occasion when Nebuchadnezzar erected a 90-foot golden statue in the plain of Dura (Daniel 3). High officials from throughout the empire gathered for the day of dedication. Every person in attendance was under an imperial decree to bow down and worship the image when the royal musicians played their instruments. The penalty for not complying with this command was death by fire. A furnace on site would serve as an execution chamber for the guilty.

The orchestra sounded, and the multitude bowed low before the statue. The ceremony seemed flawless until a group of Chaldeans approached the king and accused three young Jews of disloyalty. It was reported that they refused to worship the king's golden idol. The names of the accused were Hananiah, Mishael and Azariah in the tongue of the Hebrews. To the Babylonians, they were known as Shadrach, Meshach and Abednego.

Encouraged by the character of their fellow captive, Daniel (Belteshazzar), they refused to violate their consciences by breaking God's commandment forbidding the worship of idols (Exodus 20:3-5). They understood the penalty that would be exacted for their integrity, but it was a price they were prepared to pay. The young men displayed uncommon composure when summoned before the king. Their humble confidence must have impressed some onlookers while enraging others.

The king was willing to consider the incident a simple misunderstanding and grant his valued servants a second chance. He explained that all would be forgiven if they would bow before the golden image when the instruments sounded. But if not, they would be executed within the hour. Nebuchadnezzar concluded with this challenge: "And who is the god who will deliver you from my hands?" (Daniel 3:15).

Shadrach, Meshach and Abednego responded instantly to the king's threat. With surprising poise, they proclaimed, "[O]ur God whom we serve is able to deliver us from the burning fiery furnace, and He will deliver us from your hand, O king" (Daniel 3:17).

Burning with anger, Nebuchadnezzar ordered the furnace heated seven times hotter than usual. The defiant Jews were bound and thrown into the fire, but the soldiers in charge of the execution were also engulfed by the inferno. Nebuchadnezzar watched in astonishment at what transpired next. Instead of succumbing to the flames, Shadrach, Meshach and Abednego could be seen casually walking around in the fire. They were accompanied by a fourth person with an appearance like that of an angel. When the king ordered them out of the furnace, their hair was not singed, nor did their clothes smell of smoke.

Babylon's king blessed the name of the Hebrews' God and passed a decree calling for the death of anyone who dared to speak against the Lord. In explaining his actions, Nebuchadnezzar declared, "[T]here is no other God who can deliver like this" (Daniel 3:29). Instead of death or dismissal, Shadrach, Meshach and Abednego were promoted by the king for their courageous stand.

• **God Saves From the Lions' Den.** Sometime later, Daniel experienced a similarly harrowing incident. Because of his character and competence, he rose rapidly through the political ranks. God caused him to prosper until he was next in line to become the highest public official appointed by the king of Persia. The jealousy of his political rivals led them to conspire to unseat this foreigner who surpassed them to their embarrassment (Daniel 6).

After extensive investigation, Daniel's enemies were unable to find compromising information about his administrative affairs or his personal life. Rather than abandoning their scheme, they decided to manufacture the badly needed evidence. Settling upon religion as their point of attack, they devised an evil plan.

Feigning admiration for King Darius, they proposed a 30-day ordinance outlawing prayer to anyone but the emperor. Flattered by their proposal, Darius signed into law what they hoped would be Daniel's death warrant. Anyone who violated the order would be cast into the den of lions.

As soon as Daniel heard about the decree, he went home, opened his window toward Jerusalem, and knelt in prayer giving thanks to God. It was customary for him to pray in this manner three times every day, and he was determined not to change a thing. He refused to be coerced into denying God or living a life of deception.

When the jealous officials learned that Daniel continued his religious routine, they approached the king to inform him of the infraction. Rather than being upset with his friend, Darius was angry for allowing himself to be duped by Daniel's adversaries. He worked feverishly to find a loophole in the law, but to no avail. According to the law of the Medes and Persians, no edict signed by the king could be altered or annulled. Not even he could stop what he had set in motion.

That evening, Daniel was arrested and cast into the lions' den. A stone was placed over the opening and sealed with the signet of the king and his lords. Darius did not eat or sleep that night. At first light, he hastily returned to the den of lions and called to his friend, "Daniel, servant of the living God, has your God, whom you serve continually, been able to deliver you from the lions?" (Daniel 6:20).

The king was relieved to hear his servant's voice. Daniel explained that, because of his innocence, the Lord had sent an angel to shut the lions' mouths. After he was removed from danger, his accusers were put in his place and devoured by the lions.

Darius wrote a new decree and sent it throughout the empire. His proclamation called for people everywhere to fear the God of Daniel. He explained the bestowal of this honor by declaring, "He delivers and rescues, And He works signs and wonders In heaven and on earth, Who has delivered Daniel from the power of the lions" (Daniel 6:27).

TRUSTING GOD IN TOUGH TIMES

What God did historically for Israel by delivering them from their enemies was a sign of what He can do on man's behalf spiritually

(2 Corinthians 5:19). The Lord liberated His covenant people from the tyranny and oppression of the greatest political and military powers on earth (Egypt, Assyria, Babylonia, Persia, Rome). He is no less capable of freeing those in bondage to Satan and releasing them from the terrible consequences of slavery to sin.

In using the phrase "to Him who is able" Jude was calling to mind the witness of history to prove God's trustworthiness even in the toughest times. Just as the Lord vindicated the faith of Daniel and his friends, so Jude's readers could trust the Lord to support them in their stand for truth. When facing enemies and feeling all is lost, never underestimate God's ability to intervene providentially and bless those who put their confidence in him.

References of this kind are not limited to the Old Testament. The Lord is praised three times in the New Testament as the God who is able. In Romans 16:25, Paul glorified God as the One who is able (has the power) to establish men and women by the gospel. In Ephesians 3:20, Paul praised God in prayer as the One who is able to do "exceedingly abundantly above all that we ask or think, according to the power that works in us." The third commendation comes from the doxology in Jude's epistle.

WHAT IS GOD ABLE TO DO?

• **Keep You From Stumbling.** What did Jude want his readers to remember about God's ability? First, that He was able to keep them from falling (v. 24). The Greeks used this word to refer to a surefooted horse. God can make His people surefooted spiritually if they trust in Him.

Jude was saying that God has the means to keep His people from falling if they will avail themselves of it. God has wisdom, but men must ask for it in believing prayer (James 1:5-6). God has spiritual armor to protect His soldiers, but they must put it on (Ephesians 6:11).

The image of falling suggests that Christian living is like walking through dangerous territory en route to a predetermined destination. Those who walk with God can travel safely even in the most treacherous terrain. The psalmist declared, "He will not allow your foot to be moved" (Psalm 121:3).

When mountain climbing, the inexperienced climber is bound by a rope to his guide. If he falls, the lifeline will keep him from plunging to his death. In like manner, those who bind their lives to God will find security and peace.

A small child who goes out to play on an icy day needs a parent's supporting hand. To the child, that hand seems like a restraint, so he struggles to get free, only to fall. Suddenly, he looks at his mother's hand in a new light. It is no longer a hindrance, but a help. Unlike children, Christians never outgrow the need for their heavenly Father's guiding hand.

Saints are surrounded by stumbling blocks as they journey through life. Hypocrisy and false teaching are among the obstacles Satan places in people's way. The impediments are plentiful and difficult, yet God is able to help Christians overcome them all. How does He do it?

The providence of God is an important part of this process. Paul promised, "God is faithful, who will not allow you to be tempted beyond what you are able, but with the temptation will also make the way of escape, that you may be able to bear it" (1 Corinthians 10:13). The Lord has pledged that a person will never be tempted beyond his or her ability to say "No!" Peter added, "[T]he Lord knows how to deliver the godly out of temptations and to reserve the unjust under punishment for the day of judgment" (2 Peter 2:9). Those who are genuinely seeking a way out of potentially dangerous situations can count on God to provide an avenue of escape. It is man's responsibility to use it.

God's Word is another powerful resource to keep humans from falling. That was the idea behind Jude's letter. The Spirit was working through his writing to bolster believers and make them steady and strong. Paul said that the Word is able to build you up (Acts 20:32). James wrote that the Word is able to save a person's soul when it is received with meekness into a teachable heart (James 1:21). God's Word accomplishes these ends by providing the warnings (1 Corinthians 10:12), comfort (1 Thessalonians 4:18), encouragement (Philippians 4:13), and instruction (Acts 2:38) people need. The power of God's Word is limited only by one's failure to believe it and heed it (1 Timothy 4:16).

The knowledge of God's Word is an essential part of maintaining spiritual equilibrium. Peter exhorted Christians to add to their faith virtue, knowledge, temperance, patience, godliness, brotherly kindness and charity. In conclusion, he stated, "[F]or if you do these things you will never stumble" (2 Peter 1:5-10). In addition to divine providence and regular Bible study, Christian fellowship and believing prayer are other examples of God's means for protecting His people from spiritual collapse.

• **Present You Faultless.** Jude continued his words of adoration by stating that God is able to "present you faultless Before the presence of His glory with exceeding joy" (v. 24). The Greek word for "faultless" was used to refer to animal sacrifices that were without blemish. God deserves the best man has to offer. In his letter to the Romans, Paul used sacrifice as an analogy to describe the Christian life. Saints should strive daily to present their bodies to God in purity and holiness (Romans 12:1).

Because man, at his very best, comes short of sinless perfection, it is through Christ that God makes him faultless in the supreme sense. At life's end, every Christian hopes to appear unblemished before the presence of His glory. These words describe the awe-inspiring scene of final judgment in the presence of God.

GOD'S GLORY IN THE OLD TESTAMENT

God allowed a handful of men to glimpse His divine glory during their lifetimes on earth. Moses witnessed that splendor on Mount Horeb: "And there was under His feet as it were a paved work of sapphire stone, and it was like the very heavens in its clarity" (Exodus 24:10). After meeting with God on a different occasion, Moses' face shone so brightly it had to be covered with a veil (33:18–34:35).

The hand of the Lord came upon the prophet Ezekiel (Chapter 1) and provided him with a magnificent vision of God seated upon what appeared to be a royal chariot. Isaiah was granted a spectacular view of the Lord seated upon His throne in the temple (Isaiah 6:1-6). At Bethel, Jacob received a dream in which God stood at the head of a ladder with angels ascending and descending between heaven and earth (Genesis 28:12).

GOD'S GLORY IN THE NEW TESTAMENT

Several New Testament characters also received special revelations of divine glory. At the mount of transfiguration, Peter, James and John saw Jesus' raiment change to a brilliant white surpassing anything on earth (Mark 9:3). When Stephen was stoned, he looked up to heaven and saw the glory of God and Jesus standing at His right hand (Acts 7:55). As Saul of Tarsus traveled on the road to Damascus, Jesus appeared to him with a radiance exceeding the brilliance of the sun (9:3).

While in prison on the Isle of Patmos, John was granted what many consider to be the most extraordinary revelation of all time. His vision of the glorified, resurrected Christ gave struggling saints encouragement to endure their persecutions and sufferings.

> Then I turned to see the voice that spoke with me. And having turned I saw seven golden lampstands, and in the midst of the seven lampstands One like the Son of Man, clothed with a garment down to the feet and girded about the chest with a golden band. His head and hair were white like wool, as white as snow, and His eyes like a flame of fire; His feet were like fine brass, as if refined in a furnace, and His voice as the sound of many waters; He had in His right hand seven stars, out of His mouth went a sharp two-edged sword, and His countenance was like the sun shining in its strength. And when I saw Him, I fell at His feet as dead. (Revelation 1:12-17)

Shortly after this, John saw a door opened into heaven, and he was invited up by an angel to see the sovereign God of the universe seated upon His throne.

> Immediately I was in the Spirit; and behold, a throne set in heaven, and One sat on the throne. And He who sat there was like a jasper and a sardius stone in appearance; and there was a rainbow around the throne, in appearance like an emerald. Around the throne were twenty-four thrones, and on the thrones I saw twenty-four elders sitting, clothed in white robes; and they had crowns of gold on their heads. And from the throne proceeded lightnings, thunderings, and voices.

Seven lamps of fire were burning before the throne, which are the seven Spirits of God. Before the throne there was a sea of glass, like crystal. And in the midst of the throne, and around the throne, were four living creatures full of eyes in front and in back. (Revelation 4:2-6)

Although it is difficult to visualize God's glory, it is even harder to imagine what it will be like to stand personally before His presence. To many, it is a frightening thought, but Jude said it will be a marvelous moment for Christians. God is able to make it an exceedingly joyous occasion for the faithful (Jude 24).

After their sin in the garden, Adam and Eve felt shame and guilt in God's presence. Terrified, they hid themselves, hoping to avoid an embarrassing encounter with their Creator. Like his trembling ancestors, contemporary man senses his unworthiness to meet with God face to face. At the end of time, when all humanity stands before the judgment seat, how happy Christians will be to see that the judge to whom they must account is their own Father!

REASONS TO REJOICE

Why will that moment be a time to rejoice? Because sinful people will realize more than ever what it means to be fully and completely redeemed. When the Philippian jailer and the Ethiopian eunuch were baptized into Christ, they could not contain their emotions. They openly celebrated their conversion experience. If being forgiven is not a reason to rejoice, then what is?

Another reason to rejoice will be the great reunion that will occur at that time. The saved will be able to thank the heroes of the faith who encouraged them by their example. Saints will be reunited with loved ones who preceded them in death. Earth's greatest festivities cannot begin to compare with the celebration of the redeemed in heaven.

The renewal of the human body will also be reason for rejoicing. Sickness and death will no longer be able to intimidate God's people. Along with the reception of an incorruptible body will come the blessing of an abode that has not been adversely affected by sin. All things will be new on that glorious day.

REASONS TO PRAISE

The God who is sufficient in power and love to do all of these things is truly worthy of man's adoration. Jude exulted, "To God our Savior, Who alone is wise, Be glory and majesty, Dominion and power, Both now and forever. Amen." In this prayer of thanksgiving, Jude highlighted three traits for which the Lord is to be revered: His wisdom, His uniqueness and His saving power.

God's work in creating and maintaining the universe is the most obvious example of His wisdom. Making matter from nothing is beyond man's capability. This alone demonstrates that He is unique and without a peer.

Jude's main emphasis seems to be on the word "Savior." He envisions real dangers confronting human beings from which they are incapable of rescuing themselves. There is no one else who can save like the Lord. His wisdom in devising the scheme of redemption surpasses the glory of His work in creation. Only He could conceive a means by which to preserve His own righteousness and save sinners at the same time. Moreover, He alone is gracious and loving enough to want to help fallen mankind in the first place.

BOOSTING MORALE

If God could impart life to people and deliver them from their sins, surely He was capable of dealing with the trouble Jude's readers were facing. The unchanging, self-existent, eternal "I Am" can be counted on to bless those who earnestly contend for the faith once delivered unto the saints. He is deserving of the love, respect and worship of faithful Christians both in carefree and challenging times.

Few things are more important in warfare than morale. Soldiers who have confidence in their leader will fight with greater resolve. God's patriots are filled with unshakable trust in the goodness and power of their Commander. He promises to sustain them in their struggle and crown them with victory in the end. God has proven His reliability. The question is, "Can He depend on you?"

DISCUSSION

1. How does prayer help in times of crisis?

2. Why did Jude begin his prayer, "to Him who is able"?

3. Where in the New Testament is the Lord described as the God who is able? What thought was the writer attempting to convey?

4. How does God keep Christians from stumbling?

5. What thoughts or feelings come to your mind when you contemplate standing before the Lord's presence in glory?

6. Why will judgment be a time to rejoice for faithful Christians?

7. What evidence would you submit to prove that God is wise?

8. Share something you found meaningful from your study of the book of Jude.

9. What does it mean to you personally to be a spiritual patriot? How will you fulfill that role?

10. How has your concept of contending for the faith changed as a result of studying Jude's letter?

Epilogue
Hearts of Peace

C hristians constantly strive to promote unity and peace (Romans 12:18), but there are times when holiness demands that they resist wrongdoers (Jude 3). This is precisely what Jude did in his brief but bold letter. Jude demonstrated that it is necessary to expose error and describe the danger it presents, yet there is a difference between righteous resolve and hatemongering.

HEAVEN'S RULES FOR ENGAGEMENT

Spiritual patriots can be recognized by the elevated rules of engagement guiding their actions. Most of all, they are defined by the attitude with which they enter battle (John 13:35). First, there is an attitude of peace because they know the battle is the Lord's (Romans 16:20). Because the outcome is assured, they possess a calmness that reflects unshakable trust in God's presence and sustaining power. Ruthlessness reflects doubt and fear. Poise reflects confidence and faith (Acts 4:13).

Second, they enjoy hearts of peace toward their adversaries. For saints, the field of battle is a hate-free zone. They deplore the suffering ungodly leaders inflict on the uninformed and immature, but they are careful to maintain a distinction between the sin and the sinner. It is possible to detest a person's actions while loving his soul. A spiritual patriot knows that choosing to exclude another from his heart is a greater sin than the precipitating cause of the conflict. Failing to love is a selfish choice with severe consequences. It is the greatest wrong a human can commit.

In spiritual combat, Christians must combine composure with compassion. False teachers must be opposed, but every effort should be grounded in love rather than loathing. Compassion leaves the door open for communication and reconciliation. Callousness degrades the soul and generates sympathy for those promoting error.

THE EXAMPLE OF STEPHEN

To illustrate the power of Christlikeness in conflict, consider the stories of Stephen and Saul. Stephen was a godly man remembered for attending the needs of widows and preaching the gospel. For proclaiming truth, this spirit-filled man was murdered by an irate mob. He showered them with words of life and they rained down on him with weapons of death. The contrast is compelling. Motivated by love, Stephen risked his life to free his hearers from their sins. Motivated by hatred, they took his life to justify their sins.

As a prelude to bloodshed, they "gnashed at him with their teeth," "stopped their ears, and ran at him with one accord" (Acts 7:54b, 57b). The throng cast him outside the city and crushed the breath and life from his body. The most disturbing part of this incident was that they felt vindicated in their violence and supposed God was pleased by their brutality.

Yet even more remarkable was the calm demeanor of Christ's servant, Stephen. Rather than cowering, the council noticed an aura of peace upon his face (Acts 6:15). Rather than cursing, they heard him pray for their well-being: "Lord, do not charge them with this sin" (7:60). The angry horde hurled rocks downward. The peaceful victim lifted prayers heavenward. In both cases, the hands did what the eyes saw and the heart felt. When the heart is hardened, the eyes are darkened. Heart, eyes and hands: it is the order of life.

Stephen's prayer for his persecutors impressively mirrored the words of his Master from the cross. Although slandered, humiliated and tortured, the Son of God interceded in behalf of His judges and executioners: "Father, forgive them, for they do not know what they do"

(Luke 23:34). When people hate other people, they do not know what they do. When they looked up at Jesus, they saw a problem to be feared and eliminated. When He looked down at them, He saw people needing forgiveness and enlightenment. What each saw was a reflection of his own heart.

It would be wrong to conclude that Jesus believed no one should be held accountable for his actions. Rather, Jesus was demonstrating the spirit in which Christian warfare must be waged. Forbearing personal attacks and desiring the good of all people, Christ's followers uphold truth and oppose error with unquenchable love.

THE EXAMPLE OF SAUL

Before stoning Stephen, the executioners laid their clothes at the feet of a young man named Saul who heartily approved of their cruelty and assumed a leading role in the widening persecution (Acts 7:58; 8:1). Not content to rid his own country of Christ's followers, Saul plotted to pursue them into neighboring Damascus. His hatred knew no boundaries and continually increased rather than subsided. No matter how many men he jailed or murdered, his rage and self-righteousness grew. Not even women were spared his fury (v. 4).

On the way to Damascus, Saul was blinded by a brilliant light and confronted by the voice of the Lord. After three days of sightlessness and soul searching, a man named Ananias restored his vision and baptized him. At that moment, he was forever changed. He emerged from the water, opened his eyes, and saw the world in a different light. The cleansing of his heart revolutionized his outlook on life (Matthew 6:22-23).

When Saul became a Christian, it changed not only his religion but also his relationships. Previously, he had killed in the name of religion with an approving conscience. Now, Paul preached rather than persecuted and persuaded rather than coerced. After becoming a Christian, Paul did not merely direct his venom toward a different group. He loved his enemies and expressed genuine empathy for them (Romans 9:1-3; 10:1-2). He was a new man.

Before Saul was saved, he was very religious but also very hateful. After his conversion, he became a more righteous and compassionate person. No longer was he breathing out threats. Instead, he delighted in proclaiming faith, hope and love. This man whose eyes were opened by God joyfully embraced his mission of opening the world's eyes to the possibilities of love (Acts 26:18).

FIGHT THE GOOD FIGHT RIGHT!

When you are confident you are right, do you become wrong by the uncaring way you deal with others? Ingeniously, the devil has won more disciples through pity than persuasion. When false teachers are treated heartlessly, it fosters sympathy where logic was found wanting. Christians must earnestly *and graciously* contend for the faith.

For many people, life is one giant war zone where memories are littered with the casualties of cruelty. Be on the lookout for hatred that can seep into your soul like the deadly gases used in chemical warfare. Despite technological advancements, hate remains the most lethal of all weapons of mass destruction. Yet greater than all the hatred stockpiled in human hearts throughout the world is the love of God that radiates in His people. It is important to fight the good fight, but we must fight the good fight *right*! With hearts of peace, may we press the battle to protect the purity of the gospel, preserve the unity of the church, and promote the reign of love throughout the world.

APPENDIX A
THIRTEEN STEPS
TO SPIRITUAL VICTORY

To know victory, I must…

1. Be willing to take a stand.
2. Adapt my plans to fulfill greater needs.
3. Never use grace as an excuse for disobedience.
4. Learn from history.
5. Fill my heart with holy aspirations.
6. Choose my path carefully.
7. Make pleasing God my highest aim.
8. Be content without becoming complacent.
9. Never underestimate my enemy.
10. Prepare daily for Jesus' return.
11. Not be easily disheartened.
12. Accept personal responsibility for my spiritual growth.
13. Trust God to sustain me through trying times.

APPENDIX B
THE AUTHORSHIP OF JUDE

This book assumes that the author of Jude was the half brother of Jesus. Jude does not make that claim directly, but humility can account for this omission. It would be inappropriate to accentuate a family connection to one whose virgin birth was unique in the annals of history. Because of Jesus' distinctive position as Messiah, Jude referred to himself as Christ's servant rather than His brother. In contrast, he did not hesitate to identify himself as the brother of James. Matthew recorded that Jesus had four half brothers, two of whom were James and Jude (Matthew 13:55). The use of James' name in the opening of the epistle indicates that he was a well-known personality. The prominence of the Lord's brother as a leading figure in the church in Jerusalem fits this description (Acts 15:13; Galatians 1:19; 2:9). If a mistake was made concerning the authorship of this epistle, it has no bearing on any matter of doctrine. Still, the most likely writer of the epistle of Jude was the half brother of Christ.